ESSENTIAL PSYCHOLOGY

General Editor
Peter Herriot

A6

HUMAN MEMORY

ESSENTIAL

PSYCHOLOGY

HUMAN MEMORY

Vernon Gregg

Methuen

To my Mother

First published in 1975 by Methuen & Co Ltd
11 New Fetter Lane, London EC4P 4EE
© 1975 Vernon Gregg
Printed in Great Britain by
Richard Clay (The Chaucer Press), Ltd
Bungay, Suffolk
ISBN (hardback) 0 416 81970 2
ISBN (paperback) 0 416 81980 X

We are grateful to Grant McIntyre of Open Books Publishing Ltd
for assistance in the preparation of this Series

Contents

Editor's Introduction

We use the term memory to refer to a wide range of human activity in an everyday language; we remember what happened, how to do things, how we felt. Vernon Gregg shows how, from restricted beginnings, psychology has begun to match the richness of meaning in the everyday usage in the variety of its experimentation. Reversing the traditional text book order, he first discusses the basic store of linguistic knowledge which enables us to code our experiences for storage and retrieval: how is this semantic memory organized, and how do we retrieve information from it? Gregg then describes more traditional memory research, in which the experimenter presents material to subjects and subsequently requires its recognition or recall. How is material stored and retrieved? To what extent is it transformed from its overt physical form to its covert coded form? Do codings have to be identical at presentation and recall? What forms do they take – abstract linguistic features or visual imagery? What strategies can we use to help, and why do we forget?

This book belongs to Unit A of *Essential Psychology*, which is unified by the notion of the human being as a processor of information. Like a computer we can register information, code it, store the result, and subsequently retrieve it. Moreover, like a computer, we can use our output, or behaviour, as feedback by which to monitor our subsequent performance.

The authors in Unit A are more concerned with making generalizations about people than with exploring their individual differences. Further, they deal with personal mental processes rather than with interpersonal social processes. They also probably place more stress on the traditional scientific experiment as a source of evidence than do most of the authors of the other units.

The computer analogy is very useful for handling the sort of evidence we get from experiments. For most experiments provide the experimental subject with input or information through the senses and then subsequently measure behaviour, or output; they then make inferences about the processes which occur between the two observable events. However, the computer analogy may not be suitable for handling other situations, where there is no immediate sensory experience or no easily identifiable consequent behaviour. And some psychologists also feel that it detracts from the concept of the individual as a person who can consciously act upon and control his environment. The reader will find other general conceptual frameworks in other units. Coming to terms with a variety of explanatory frameworks decreases our confidence in psychology as a mature science; but perhaps it is best that we should be honest about what we don't know.

Essential Psychology as a whole is designed to reflect the changing structure and function of psychology. The authors are both academics and professionals, and their aim has been to introduce the most important concepts in their areas to beginning students. They have tried to do so clearly, but have presented psychology as a developing set of views of man, not as a body of received truth. Readers are not intended to study the whole series in order to 'master the basics'. Rather, since different people may wish to use different theoretical frameworks for their own purposes, the series has been designed so that each title stands on its own. But it is possible that if the reader has read no psychology before, he will enjoy individual books more if he has read the introductions (A1, B1, etc.) to the units to which they belong. Readers of the units concerned with applications of psychology (E and F) may benefit from reading all the introductions.

A word about references in the text to the work of other writers – e.g. 'Smith, 1974'. These occur where the author feels he must acknowledge (by name) an important concept or some crucial evidence. The book or article referred to will be listed in the references (which double as name index) at the back of the book. The reader is invited to consult these sources if he wishes to explore topics further. A list of general further reading is also to be found at the back of each book.

We hope you enjoy psychology.

Peter Herriot

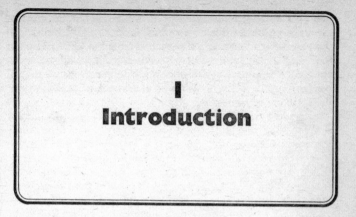

I
Introduction

What is memory?

What is understood by the word *memory*? If someone claims to 'have a good memory for names' it is understood that he can usually name people correctly some time after being introduced to them. When the naming is correct the person is said to *remember* the name; when the name cannot be produced the person is said to *forget*. In this sense the word *memory* implies an *ability* to name people, but it is often used as though it refers to a *thing*, i.e. some mechanism which is responsible for remembering and forgetting. The expression 'my memory failed me' seems to reflect this view; when memory works well we remember, when it fails we forget. The expression 'I have many happy memories' illustrates another common use of the word *memory*. By this it is understood that the speaker can re-experience certain aspects of past events. For example, he may be able to remember what the church looked like on his wedding day, that is, he may be able to produce a 'mental image' of the scene. He may also be able to re-experience some of his emotional sensations at the time. Almost certainly he will remember the date of the occasion. When used in this way *memory* refers to *what* is remembered.

The scientific investigation of memory is directed towards answering such questions as 'How do we remember?', 'What can we remember?' and 'Why do we forget?'. If there is only one word to refer to several aspects of the topic under investigation it becomes difficult to think about it clearly and impossible to communicate with others about it. Even if only the 'mechanism' of memory is considered it soon becomes apparent that this consists of several different parts each of which requires a distinguishing name. A simple analogy will help make this point clear.

Consider an ordinary tape recorder which records sounds made at one time and reproduces them at a later time when required. The recorder has several main parts. The microphone changes the sound waves in the air into electricity which is fed into a magnet and the changes in magnetism, corresponding to changes in sound, are recorded on a magnetic tape. The sound is reproduced by passing the magnetized tape over a pick-up head which changes the patterns of magnetism back into electric current and this is passed into the loudspeakers which convert it into sound – a reproduction of the original. This can all be summed up as three stages: (1) the sound waves are converted or *coded* into patterns of magnetism which are recorded on the tape; (2) these magnetic *codes* are *stored* on the tape over a period of time; (3) the codes are picked up from the tape (without wiping them off), and reconverted or *decoded* into the corresponding sounds. The tape stores sufficient *information* to reproduce the sound. The term *information* will be used frequently in this book so its meaning must be clear. The magnetic codes on the tape 'instruct' the loudspeakers what to do to reproduce the sound and so *information* refers to *instructions*. A postal address contains information because it instructs the postman where to deliver the letter.

Memory systems and processes. The analogy between the tape recorder and memory is straightforward. When past events are remembered it is equivalent to replaying the recorder: the tape has its counterpart in the *memory store*. For events to be re-experienced they must be recorded in this store, stored over an interval of time, and retrieved from, i.e. taken out of, the store when needed. Whatever has to be done to record the experiences in the store is known as the *storage process*, and whatever has to be done to retrieve the information from the store is known as the *retrieval process*. We have already identi-

10

fied several smaller components or sub-processes which make up the storage process. These are the recording of information in the store, or *learning*, e.g. learning that 'this person's name is John'; and keeping this information in the store, i.e. *retaining* it over a period of time. The *processes* involved in remembering are carried out by the *memory system*. To return to our analogy, the complete tape recorder is the sound-reproducing *system* which carries out the processes of recording and reproducing sounds.

It is possible to pursue the analogy too far; the human memory system is far more complicated than the tape recorder. For example, the human memory system does not function in a *passive* manner merely taking in what it is given. Instead, it is *dynamic*, capable of deciding what is worth storing and how it should be stored. However, the analogy will suffice to clarify one more point which is concerned with *forgetting*. The quality of reproduction obtained with a tape recorder depends on the functioning of all the components in the system. A poor reproduction, or none at all, may be due to poor functioning of the recording components; the tape may shrink as time passes or the recording may be interfered with by some other source of magnetism; or the pick-up head and sound production equipment may be working poorly. In a similar way failure to remember may be due to failure to *learn*, the codes in the memory store may deteriorate due to biological activity in the brain, or because future learning interferes with them; or there may be a failure of the retrieval process.

Learning and memory

It is not possible to remember something unless it has been learned! Why then do we have two separate books in this series to deal with Learning (A3 of *Essential Psychology*) and Human Memory? The reason is that both topics are large and complex and it is *convenient* to deal with them separately. *Learning* tends to cover the first part of what we have called the storage process, that is, putting information into the memory store, while *memory* tends to be concerned with retention and retrieval. A simple example will help to make this distinction.

Suppose a mother wishes her son to buy ten items of

groceries. Having no paper and pencil she tells him what the items are. She then makes him *recall* them, i.e. repeat them to her, just to make sure he gets them correct. As may be expected, he manages to recall only four of them, so she repeats the list and this time he recalls six. The next time he recalls nine, and then ten. The boy is said to be *learning* the list; he is acquiring the ability to recall the whole list. Research which is labelled *learning* is generally concerned with whatever speeds up or slows down this acquisition of ability. When the boy gets to the shop he can only recall nine of the ten items; he has forgotten one. Suppose he had met some friends on the way to the shop and had been delayed. Now his performance at recalling the items could be down to seven, or if the delay had been very long perhaps he will recall only five. Why he forgets some of the items and how he remembers others falls into the domain of *memory*.

The distinction between learning and memory is not a clear one. Some of the situations discussed in this book may appear to be concerned more with learning than with memory but this is unimportant provided insight is gained into one or both areas of investigation.

Everyday memory

Memory is involved when experiences at one time affect behaviour at a future time. As such, memory is involved in every form of behaviour both *overt*, which can be observed by others; and *covert*, which is known only to the individual, e.g. usually thinking or dreaming. It is not possible to understand language unless we have learned the meanings of words and have them stored away for reference. Nor can we recognize and deal appropriately with objects unless we can draw on representations of past experiences to indicate their properties and uses. Skills such as walking, and the images of our dreams, all depend on the retained effects of previous experiences. The following scheme is offered as an aid to classifying the various situations in which memory is involved. It is not exhaustive and the reader may be able to devise other, more adequate schemes!

Semantic memory. This is involved in the use of language which requires knowledge of the meanings of words and the rules by which they are combined into sentences. An example of the contents of semantic memory is provided by the rule that the word *John* is a name appropriate for a male. This type of information is stored over long periods of time, usually for most of the individual's life.

Factual memory. Storage and use of knowledge of a specific kind, e.g. '*John* is *this* boy's name'. One's own name and the dates of birthdays are further examples.

Episodic memory. This is represented by the situation in which one remembers 'I *did* post that letter this morning?'. It is memory for episodes or events. The important point about this type of situation is that it involves things which are already familiar, such as a letter. What is retained is information about events involving the letter.

Skills. Talking, walking, driving a car, playing soccer are all skills which have to be learned. Once learned we are able to perform them without relearning. The necessary information must be stored in the memory system until required.

Imagery. Most people are able to form 'mental images' of faces or of scenes from the past. These images form the content of dreams, both when awake (day-dreams) and when asleep. Since these images occur without the presence of the faces and scenes they represent, they must be formed from information contained in the memory system.

Forgetting. Failure to remember is a frustrating but normal part of life. Forgetting becomes more evident in old age, and certain types of brain damage lead to various sorts of memory failure. Forgetting can be purposeful, as when an individual does not wish to remember a tragic event.

The scientific study of memory

Scientific investigation is directed towards understanding natural events, that is, finding orderly patterns in them. The identification of patterns of events can reveal *cause and effect* relationships between them. This in turn, enables future events to be predicted and taken account of as, for instance, when study of weather patterns enables the occurrence of hurricanes to be predicted. It also enables the causal events to be manipulated to produce desired effects, as for occurred example when malaria was linked causally to mosquito bites; malaria can be eradicated by exterminating the mosquito! Scientific investigation involves controlled observation (experiments) and the discovery of relationships between events (construction of theories). In practice these two activities alternate, possibly some observations are made first and a theory constructed to explain them in terms of causes and effects. Further observations may not fit the theory and so it has to be modified, and this suggests more experiments which must be run to test it. These points are dealt with more fully in A1 and by Popper (1959). The activities of controlled observation and theory construction are now dealt with briefly as they relate to the study of memory.

Experimentation

Speculation about *how* we remember and *why* we forget has gone on for thousands of years but the experimental study of memory did not begin until Ebbinghaus undertook his work in Germany in 1875. These investigations are notable for their emphasis on the two essentials of experimentation, *control* and *measurement*. In one experiment Ebbinghaus, using himself as *subject*, recorded the time it took to learn lists of thirteen nonsense syllables (e.g. GUF) until he could recall all of them. Then after intervals of time ranging from twenty minutes to thirty-one days he noted how long it took to learn them again to one perfect recall of the whole list. As would be expected, it took longer to relearn the lists as the interval increased and hence as more of the original learning was forgotten. However, the important point is that *performance* was *measured* accurately and at specified time intervals. The conditions of the experiment were *controlled* and *reported* together with the results, and so well was this done that when the conditions have been repeated by others very similar results have been obtained.

One aspect of the control in Ebbinghaus' experiment is worth discussing in detail. He used nonsense syllables as the material to be remembered because he wished to equate all the lists for learning difficulty; this was necessary because different lists were tested at different intervals. Had words been used there would almost certainly have been differences in ease of learning because some words are more familiar than others, and they differ in many other ways which, as we shall see in Chapter 6, affect the ease with which they can be learned. If the words had differed in difficulty there would have been the distinct possibility that the easy lists were tested at short intervals and the difficult lists at long intervals. This would appear to show that forgetting increased as the interval increased, whereas the effect might have been produced by list difficulty. The effects of difficulty and the effects of interval are *confounded* (see A8) in such a situation: it is not possible to separate the effects of one from the effects of the other.

Ebbinghaus chose verbal materials (letter sequences) because they are easy to classify as correct or incorrect *responses*; the subject either recalls them correctly or not. Other forms of memory content such as visual imagery are not directly open to observation by the experimenter who must rely on the subjects' reports of what is experienced. This choice by Ebbinghaus started a long tradition of work involving verbal materials to the detriment of research into other forms of memory such as imagery. The emphasis of this book reflects this situation.

Theories of memory

The study of memory is concerned with situations in which experiences occurring at one time have effects on behaviour at a later time. How is the experience carried forward in time? In order to understand such situations in the scientific sense we have to accept that one event cannot affect another event at a different time without some linking sequence of causes and effects.

It seems rather obvious that the means whereby experiences are transmitted through time reside in the organic materials which make up the individual who is doing the remembering (see A2). This view is supported by ample evidence that damage by disease, accident or ageing to certain parts of the brain have specific effects (usually detrimental) on the functioning of the memory system (see Williams, 1970). There has also been a vast amount of research into the working of single cells and small groups of cells in the brain. These investigations have made use of highly sophisticated techniques which allow electrical recordings to be taken from individual cells, or detection of chemical activity at the junctions between cells. Unfortunately these investigations have not provided much help in understanding how skills, events, language rules etc. are remembered because the cells of the brain do not work independently. Remembering a particular event probably involves a large number of cells and it is necessary to understand how they work together if we are to explain memory for *integrated* portions of experience in terms of cell activity; the necessary organization of the cells is too complicated for scientists to deal with at present.

Most theories of memory are what may be called 'as if' theories. They help us understand the cause and effect relationships between observations in memory situations by borrowing explanations from other fields of science which we understand already. Because of this, 'as if' theories are referred to as *models*. The tape recorder mentioned earlier illustrates a model because memory was discussed 'as if' it worked like a tape recorder. Plato (425–348 BC) proposed a model of memory based on wax writing tablets. He observed that memories become less distinct as time passes rather like the impressions on a wax tablet. In this model the act of writing is equivalent to learning the material, the wax tablet represents a memory store, and reading the inscriptions represents the attempt to recall the material. Forgetting is attributed to changes taking place in the memory store, i.e. fading as time passes.

Computers have been an obvious choice for recent models of memory because they are very competent at storing a large amount of information and retrieving it when required. The information is contained in a store which consists of many *locations* or small stores usually holding information in the form of electric charges. Each location has an *address* by means of which it can be found and the information in it inspected or changed. Suppose one location contains a bank balance and the customer wishes to know its contents. The address and the instruction to retrieve the contents must be given to the computer by typing them, usually onto punched cards; they are then changed into codes which the computer can understand. When the contents have been found they are printed on paper by a typewriter controlled by the computer. Here we see the storage and retrieval processes mentioned earlier in connection with human memory. Indeed the terms were borrowed from computer science.

The usefulness of the computer model is not restricted to the distinction between storage and retrieval processes. Computers can manipulate the information they store, e.g. they can make decisions about it, and do arithmetic with numbers. They are able to 'learn' the rules to do these operations; that is, once the instructions have been put into the computer they can be used without repeating them again. By 'learning' rules and applying them the computer is able to carry out some of the tasks which are known as *thinking* in the human.

The experimental subject
There is always the danger that psychologists who use models to explain their experimental results will forget that models are only *as if* theories. The use of them does not imply that the people from whom the results came (the experimental *subjects*) *are* machines. It is necessary to realize, however, that human subjects are members of the animal kingdom; they are organic systems. Things go wrong with them, they differ from each other in many ways, and there are limitations on what they can achieve, both physical and mental. Activities such as learning, reasoning, using language, and remembering are known as *cognitive* activities, and the speed with which they can be carried out is limited just as the speed with which an individual can run is limited: the *capacity* to carry out *cognitive* work is limited.

The subjects of a memory experiment bring with them their individual characteristics, e.g. personal needs and emotional reactions, sex, age, educational background, intelligence, language ability. It is the job of the experimenter to ensure that these individual characteristics are not *confounded,* i.e. mixed up, with the variables of experimental interest (see A1 and A8). Try as one may, it is not possible to study *pure* memory, i.e. memory unaffected by previous learning. It has been made clear already that if the subject is asked to remember a list

17

of words, he does not have to learn what the words are; they are already in his vocabulary, his semantic memory (see p. 13). What he has to learn is that these particular words, out of all the words he knows, appeared in the list. He performs this *episodic* memory task (see p. 13) by making use of his experiences with the words prior to the experiment, as will be shown in Chapters 6 and 8.

Any memory experiment, then, is concerned with the behaviour of subjects who already have a vast amount of information stored inside them. Chapters 2, 3 and 4 describe some of the methods which have been devised to examine this information.

Experimental procedures
For the sake of simplicity the experimental procedures will be described when verbal materials are used, but the corresponding procedures for pictures, events, or tones, etc. are easy to construct from the examples given here.

The procedures used to investigate episodic memory follow a single, general plan: (1) presentation of the materials to be remembered; (2) retention interval; (3) test. The presentation is usually carried out by presenting the items one at a time at a specified rate which can range from about four items per second to one item every ten seconds, depending on the experimenter's interests. Presenting the items one at a time gives the experimenter control over the order in which the subject encounters them and also the time he has between items. This does not ensure that he spends an equal time attending to them; he may miss one out and spend twice as long learning another! Retention intervals ranging from fractions of a second to years have been employed in memory research. The interval between presentation and test can be left empty, so that subjects may pursue any activity they wish, or it may be filled with a task which prevents them *rehearsing* the items (repeating the items to themselves and trying to learn them further). The tests fall into two broad categories, *recall* and *recognition*. In a recall test the subject must produce (spoken or written) the items which were presented to him. In recognition, the items which appeared in the presentation list are mixed up with some *new* items which did not appear in the list and the subject must indicate whether each

18

item given at test is *new* or *old* (one of the originals). There are many variations of these basic procedures, some of which are encountered in this book. They are described when they occur.

The procedures outlined above are relevant to the study of episodic memory. When semantic memory is of interest there is no need for the presentation stage nor the retention interval; the aspects of memory which are of interest already exist inside the subject having been established during his life-time before the experiment. Tests of semantic memory include word-association tests in which the subjects produce the first word which occurs to them in response to the stimulus word, and procedures which measure the time taken to answer questions such as 'Is a canary a bird?'. Tests of this type are discussed in Chapters 2 and 3.

The plan of the book

The organization of the book reflects the view that the experimental subject brings to the laboratory a vast amount of information which he utilizes to perform the tasks set him. Chapters 2, 3 and 4 describe some of the procedures used to examine the content of the subject's long-standing store of information and the way the storage is organized, also the ways in which information is retrieved from it. Chapters 5–8 are concerned with episodic memory: they examine what is known about the way in which episodes in the experiment are recorded in the memory system. Special emphasis is placed on the role of semantic memory in this and the way in which the necessary retrieval is accomplished. Some explanations of failure to remember are considered in Chapter 9.

It is not possible to cover the whole field of memory research in one book, so many interesting and important areas have had to be omitted. The emphasis on memory for verbal materials, which reflects the pattern of research over many years, is achieved at the expense of motor skills, pictorial stimuli, sounds etc. Also sadly neglected are the differences in memory capacity between individuals. Even so, the study of verbal memory itself is limited, the most noticeable omission being memory for sentences (but see Ch. 6, A7) and stories. However, it is hoped that the content and organization of the book will help the reader appreciate the *experimental* approach to the study of memory and the manner in which conclusions about memory functions are derived from the results.

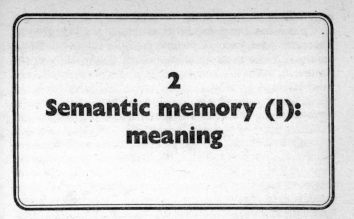

2
Semantic memory (I): meaning

Human behaviour is dominated by the use of language, that is, the use of symbols to represent ideas, events, objects, actions, feelings, relations and all other aspects of experience. By agreeing on what each symbol refers to and the manner in which the symbols may be combined into sequences individuals are able to communicate with each other. In order to understand the meaning of the sentence 'The man hit the boy' the reader must know to what sort of objects in the world *boy* and *man* refer to; also to what action *hit* refers. In addition the rules for combining the words must be known so that the reader knows whether it is the man or the boy who was doing the hitting. The words alone convey nothing about who is performing the action since they can be rearranged to convey an entirely different set of events such as 'The man the boy hit'. The speaker of the sentence, wishing to communicate the event, faces the task of finding words corresponding, by the conventions of the language, to the objects and actions of the situation and forming them into a sequence which the listener can interpret correctly. In both cases the individuals must possess a set of rules stating what particular symbols refer to and the ways in which they may be formed into sequences, and these rules must be stored in a fairly permanent memory store because once learned they persist throughout the individual's life.

The study of *semantic memory* is concerned with the roles assigned to the linguistic symbols, with their *meanings*. The

21

basic unit of language is the *word* because it is the smallest unit which has a meaning or set of meanings allocated to it. There are several ways in which the term *meaning* may be used and these must be distinguished before we proceed further. A useful distinction can be made between what the word refers to by linguistic convention and what the word refers to for a particular individual. The former sense is represented by the entries of authoritative dictionaries and the latter sense by the way in which the individual uses and responds to the word. To take an example, the word *paradigm* conventionally refers to a *plan, pattern* or *example*, these being the entries in a dictionary. However, for a particular individual this word may have no meaning, never having been encountered or used. Again, for one individual the word *bread* may have only one meaning, 'kneaded, moistened flour leavened with yeast and baked in an oven'. For another person it may have this meaning and also that of 'money' in which case the word is polysemous, having more than one meaning. Such words are known as *homographs*, having one spelling but more than one meaning.

The interpretation of homographs in sentences is facilitated either by the structure of the sentence or by our knowledge of the world. For example, interpretation of the word *fish* as a noun is necessary in the sentence 'He caught the fish', but it functions as a verb in 'He went to fish'. No such help is given by the form of the sentence in the interpretation of 'This is a yard': knowledge of the context in which the sentence is uttered is necessary to distinguish between a closed space and a unit of length as the meaning of *yard*. It is important to distinguish between the meanings of words and the rules according to which they may be formed into sequences. The latter, known as *syntactic rules*, must be known if speaker and listener are to interpret the sentence in the same way, and they therefore take a central place in theories of sentence production. One such theory, due to Chomsky, has been referred to by Judith Greene in A7 of this series (as well as in a fuller treatment in an earlier book [Greene, 1972]). Basically what Chomsky proposes is that sentences are constructed from a central plan or kernel representing the ideas that must be communicated. For example, the situation represented by 'The man hit the boy' is basically expressed by *something performing an action.* The syntactic rules state that this situation may be expressed as a *noun phrase* followed by a *verb phrase*. The verb phrase can itself be expanded into a verb (hit) and a noun phrase (the boy). Having generated the structure of the sentence in this way the next process is the retrieval, from the word store, of the words which fit the objects and actions of the situation being communicated and these are then entered into the sentence structure. However, alternative theories exist which place less emphasis on the grammatical structure and more on the meaning of sentences.

The use of language is a two-way process; the speaker or writer must be able to translate his ideas into the correct symbols and to emit them in a grammatical form; the listener or reader must be able to interpret the symbols appropriately. In order to do this both speaker and listener must have an extensive store of information about word meanings and syntactic rules, together with the means of getting to this information when it is required. In other words, the memory system must perform two functions; it must enable the meanings attached to a word to be retrieved from the word store and also, given the need to communicate a particular meaning, it must enable the appropriate word to be emitted as a response. In the first of these situations it functions like a dictionary; find the word in the memory store and a list of meanings is attached to it. In the second situation it functions like an encyclopaedia; it will enable a label to be given to a meaning. Alternatively, in this second situation a better analogy may be that of a thesaurus in which words are grouped together according to their meanings rather than alphabetically as in a dictionary.

A simple model for a system which can function as both dictionary and encyclopaedia is provided by a certain type of filing card which has a series of holes punched round the edge. Each hole is allocated to a particular topic and if the item on the card is irrelevant to that topic then the card is punched further as shown in Figure 2.1. Suppose each card represents a word and that these are stored in alphabetical order. If the meaning of *man* is required the card can be found by searching alphabetically and the punching of the card inspected. If, however, a word denoting a human, adult male is required the word *man* can be retrieved by inserting a needle into the deck of cards through the *male* hole and lifting. This will pull out all words with *male* features. These cards can then be sorted for *adult* and then for *human* features. This will yield a small set of cards amongst which will be that for *man*.

The contents of this chapter and the next one can be summed up by three questions: What is stored in semantic memory? How is it stored? How is it retrieved? The first of

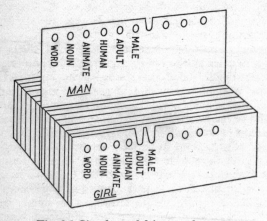

Fig. 2.1 *Simple model for word storage*

these questions will be tackled by looking at methods which have been employed to assess the responses, verbal, imaginal and physiological, which word stimuli provoke. The two questions are investigated by indirect means usually based on the time taken to answer questions about the meanings of words. It is not clear whether the functions of dictionary and encyclopaedia are carried out by separate parts of semantic memory or by a single system. If the latter is true then an extensive amount of cross-referencing is necessary. It is the large amount of information held in semantic memory and the extent of the interrelatedness of it which presents the formidable challenge to the student of semantic memory but, if this were not enough, the challenge is intensified by the speed with which the human cognitive system can interpret incoming sequences of linguistic symbols and convert ideas into outgoing sequences. The rate at which this can be done suggests that the input, storage and retrieval systems must be economically organized and because of this there has been great emphasis on techniques which measure the speed at which semantic processes can be carried out. These techniques will receive consideration later, in Chapter 3; but first, approaches to the study of word meaning will be dealt with.

Word meaning

Hearing or seeing a word can have a range of effects on a person depending on his experience of the word and the context in which it is presented. The word *fire* on a cold, wet night may provoke a visual image of home and feelings of warmth, but the same word heard in a crowded cinema will result in fear responses and action directed towards evacuating the building. It is convenient to consider the effects a word has on a subject as its *meaning*, which must then include emotional responses, imagery and verbal responses. This definition of word meaning is not agreed by everyone: some theorists maintain that *meaning* refers to the contents and organization of semantic memory which determine the responses which follow a given stimulus or collection of stimuli. This distinction will not be pursued here because it is sufficient to recognize that the two are intimately related, the contents and organization of memory being inferred from the relations of responses to the stimuli which provoke them. Of course, it is only the stimuli and responses which can be observed and then only in an objective way. Just what the stimuli signify for a particular subject must be inferred from the types of responses they provoke. This has led to a distinction being made between the *nominal* stimulus as defined by the experimenter and the *functional* stimulus as it affects the subject.

Some responses to words are not observable by anyone other than the subject but they may be described by him. Because of the problem involved in classifying effects such as visual imagery, experiments on meaning have concentrated on verbal meaning, verbal responses being more easily classified, superficially at least. Imagery is dealt with in Chapter 4; methods of measuring other aspects of word meaning are discussed in the rest of this chapter.

Connotative meaning

Words come to acquire pleasant and unpleasant meanings as a result of experiences in life. For a particular individual the word *John* may have no greater significance than that it is a proper noun appropriate for a male. For someone else it may refer to a loving and devoted husband. These two individuals would certainly give different responses if asked what they 'felt' about the word. It is difficult for most people to assess their feelings and to describe them to the experimenter in an ordered way. Because of this it is best to give some guidance to the subject and elicit his descriptions in an orderly and easily classified form. Osgood incorporates these features into his *Semantic Differential* method of assessing meaning (see Osgood, 1953). The method requires the subject to rate the stimulus word on a number of 7-point scales each representing a bipolar dimension such as good-bad, beautiful-ugly, pleasant-unpleasant etc. He is required to rate the word using the 7 points by giving a response of $+3$ if he rates it 'very good', 0 if he rates it neither good nor bad, and -3 if he rates it 'very bad', and so on for each dimension. When all the ratings have been obtained a profile of the word can be obtained by plotting the scores on a graph as shown in Figure 2.2. This shows a fictitious profile for the word *baby*.

Osgood used as many as fifty dimensions to obtain profiles but he found that it was not necessary to have this many. Indeed, since some of the dimensions are very similar, e.g. active-passive and lively-still, they show similar scores on most words for most subjects. By looking at the dimensions which show the same patterns of responses Osgood was able to distinguish three principal dimensions, *evaluation* (good-bad etc.), *activity* (activity-passive etc.) and *potency* (strong-weak). Interestingly common words tend to be rated high on evaluation, i.e. they are pleasant and at first glance this seems to indicate that there are more good things going on in the world than bad ones. Unfortunately this need not be the case because there are many more uncommon words than common ones!

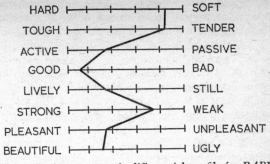

Fig. 2.2 *Fictitious semantic differential profile for BABY*

Denotative meaning

Denotative meanings are definitions of the objects, events etc. to which words refer. As such they are the meanings listed in dictionaries. The number of dictionary meanings listed for a word is usually referred to as its *dm* value. Words with *dm* greater than 1 are known as homographs as we have already seen earlier in this chapter. Where a word has more than one meaning it can be interpreted by the subject in any of those ways and, as we will see later, this can lead to difficulties in remembering these words because they may be interpreted according to one meaning when they are learned but according to another meaning when memory is being tested later on.

Associative meaning

The term *association* was used by the British Associationists of the eighteenth and nineteenth centuries (e.g. Locke and Hobbes) to refer to the temporal relations between ideas. If one idea leads to another they were said to be associated and this sequence in the occurrence of ideas was held to correspond with the ordering, in the world, of the events to which the ideas refer. The term association defines the likelihood that one idea follows another, rather than the mechanism producing the sequence. Just as a stimulus word may elicit images or feelings of pleasure in the subject so it may lead to verbal responses which must be considered part of the word's meaning according to our definition of meaning. The *method of free association* is one means of investigating meaning by obtaining spontaneous verbal responses to stimulus words. The procedure generally consists of presenting a stimulus word and requiring the subject to respond with the first word he 'thinks of'. Two main measures of *associative meaning* are available; the first response given may be taken as an indication of the most dominant aspect of the word's meaning, while the whole set of responses given to one word in a specified time may be considered as a profile of the meaning.

Amount of meaning. If *meaning* refers to the set of effects the word has on a subject then if a large number of associative responses can be made to the word it indicates an extensive meaning. Noble developed this idea by using controlled association to measure the number of associative responses elicited by a given word in one minute (Noble, 1963). In this procedure the subject is given a sheet of paper on which the same stimulus word is written many times. He reads the stimulus and writes down the first word which 'occurs' to him. Immediately he then reads the word again and writes down the next word which occurs to him and continues for one minute. The purpose of having him read the stimulus word before making each response is to prevent chained associations such as *cat-dog*; *dog-bone*, rather than *cat-dog*; *cat-mouse*. Noble refers to the average number of associations given to a word by a sample of subjects as its *meaningfulness* and it is important to distinguish between this and *word-meaning* (which includes emotional and imaginal responses) and *denotative meaning* (referred to above).

Distribution of associative responses. The types of responses obtained in free association tests depend very much on the speed with which the responses are emitted. If the subject is allowed to take his time then they tend to reflect the occurrence of vivid imagery and rich verbal relations, and may well give an indication of the deeper aspects of the subject's personality – what may be called the psychodynamics of the individual. Because of this, these slow responses are of interest in a clinical setting where attempts are made to uncover problems the patient may be experiencing in coping with life. When required to respond fairly quickly the subject produces

28

responses which are more directly related to the stimulus words in terms of semantic relations, e.g. coming from the same taxonomic category (e.g. *cat-dog*: both are animals), synonyms (e.g. *big-large*), the same parts of speech etc. Under instructions to respond as quickly as possible subjects typically produce 'clang associations' such as *can-cat* or *hat-mat*. This variety of stimulus-response relations suggests that subjects employ different rules for generating responses depending on how much time they have and what they consider to be required by the experimenter or clinician. The discussion which follows will be restricted by the experimenter to the moderately fast associative responses because semantic relations are of interest here.

One of the most striking aspects of word associations is the almost complete absence of stimulus-response pairs which reflect the sequential characteristics of linguistic utterances. Rather than obtaining the pair *meal-was* as would be expected from common utterances such as 'the *meal was* awful', the response to *meal* is likely to be *food*. This suggests that associations are not simply habits acquired by the frequent use of linguistic rules of a different kind to generate their responses. Such a notion fits in well with present theories of the way in which linguistic sequences are generated. The weight of opinion currently rejects the idea that sentences are produced as chains of stimulus-response pairs with each word eliciting the next as a conditioned response (see A7). This approach maintains that the speaker learns the permitted sequences in the language by being rewarded for producing one word after another in the way that a rat learns to press a bar in order to get a food reward (see A3). This theory, whose main proponent is B. F. Skinner, is readily discredited because it cannot account for the production of sequences which the speaker has not uttered nor encountered before and cannot have been rewarded for. It has already been pointed out that one current theory, that of Chomsky, maintains that sentences are generated from a *kernel* or central idea: the appropriate sentence structure is formed and words inserted into it. The words have to be obtained from the word store or *lexicon* and this is only possible if each word is identified by a set of features which correspond to its meaning and permit selection of words possessing the semantic and syntactic characteristics appropriate for the sentence. Thus the word *man* is represented by a list of features which includes [+Noun, +Animate, +Human, +Adult, +Male] where the + indicates that the word meaning contains the properties of being Male, Adult etc. Clark (1970) shows how this explanation of sentence production provides an attractive explanation of word association data.

Clark points out that in order to fulfil the requirements of a word association test the subject must complete three processes: (1) interpret the stimulus, (2) decide on the sort of rule to use in generating the response, and (3) apply that rule. The important point about Clark's explanation is the observation that subjects tend to use rules which involve a minimum change in the features of the stimulus word; this is essentially a principle of least cognitive effort. For example, if the subject's interpretation of the stimulus *man* is represented by the list of features [+Noun, +Animate, +Adult, +Male] then the easiest way of generating a response would be to change the lowest, that is most specific feature to the opposite sign. Since the + sign indicates 'possessing the properties of' the − sign indicates possession of properties at the opposite end of the dimension represented by the feature, and changing [+Man] to [−Man] produces the set of features defining *woman* which is indeed a common response to *man*. (The reader is referred to papers accompanying Clark's in the book edited by Lyons for further description of *features*.) Simply deleting the feature [+Man] from *man* will produce the response *adult*, again a common response to *man*.

The rules discussed above do not involve any changes in the grammatical class of the words; both stimulus and response belong to the same class. A further set of rules does involve a change of class as in the stimulus-response pair *young-child*. Here the rule seems to involve addition of features rather than changing the sign or deletion: if the feature [+Human] is added to the features of *young* the result is indeed *child*. Despite the fact that sequences such as *young-child* appear in normal speech it is best to consider that they occur in word association tests as a result of the application of the principle of least-feature-change rather than simple sequential habit formation. This is because many such stimulus-response pairs do not occur directly in speech, e.g. *cut-knife*.

Clark's view of the free association test is that it is a game in which the subjects are free to select their own rules for generating responses and this they do usually in ways which involve the least amount of cognitive processing while respecting the experimenter's desire to avoid superficial, clang relations.

Associative structural meaning. Clark's analysis of the rules used to generate associative responses reflects the findings that stimulus-response pairs represent similarities and differences in objects and events in the world. Deese (1965) has expressed the view that this is to be expected since the knowledge of such similarities and differences is essential for survival. He has also gone further and suggested that it is not particularly informative to look at the responses made to individual words if we wish to explore the way in which semantic memory is organized. Instead, the similarities and differences between the meanings of different words must be determined and the resulting set of relations should indicate the overall structure of semantic memory in terms of associative meaning.

One way in which the associative meaning of a particular word may be assessed is to give it as a stimulus word to a large number of subjects and record their first, dominant response. For example, a typical result is provided by the stimulus word *needle* to which 16 per cent of subjects gave the response *thread* in an experiment using students as subjects. *Pin* was given by 15 per cent, *sew* by 14 per cent, *point* by 4 per cent, and so on. The distribution of responses gives some indication of the meaning of the word *needle* for this group of subjects taken together. Tables showing the distributions of responses for various words and populations of subjects are available (Postman and Keppel, 1970).

Deese argued that semantic memory could only be investigated profitably by looking at the relations between the meanings of words assessed by the method just described. He maintained that the distinction between the meaning of a word and the relation of that meaning to the meaning of another word is important because it is possible for two words never to elicit each other as associative responses but nevertheless to have very similar associative meaning. For example, *piano* and *symphony* do not elicit each other but they both elicit *note, song, sound, noise, music* and *orchestra*. By contrast, *soft* and *loud* elicit each other very frequently but have no responses in common.

Deese assessed the relations between some word meanings by firstly obtaining a single associative response to the word *butterfly* from a group of subjects. Other subjects were given these responses from the first group as stimulus words and these second sets of responses examined for common members. For example, *moth* and *insect* were responses given to *butterfly* by the first group and both of these elicit a relatively large number of common responses; *insect* and *spring*, however, share no responses with each other. The overlap of the associative response sets of the two stimulus words defines the relationship between their meanings; if they share a large proportion of their responses then they are similar in associative meaning. It is possible to group together stimulus words which have similar associative meanings and when this is done with the *butterfly* set Deese found several clusters of stimulus words which he classified as (1) animate creation, i.e. bees, flies, bug, wing, bird; and (2) inanimate, i.e. sky, yellow, spring. A second method of classification gave (3) summer, sunshine, garden, flower; and (4) blue, sky, yellow, colour. The free association procedure offers a way of looking at the organization of semantic memory as a whole and of comparing the meaning of particular pairs of words, and its importance is emphasized by the fact that the associative relationships amongst words in a list gives a good indication of how easy the list will be to remember, as we will see in Chapter 6.

Meaningfulness of nonsense items. It no doubt appears paradoxical to refer to the meaningfulness of items which are also referred to as nonsense and hence meaningless. The paradox vanishes when it is recalled that meaningfulness is defined as the number of associations produced in response to the item in a given time, and this is quite different from the denotative *meanings* of an item. A nonsense item may have meaningfulness but not meanings! Nonsense items, as used in memory research, fall into various classes but the most frequently used are *trigrams*, that is, three letter items such as XYJ which contains three consonants and abreviated to a CCC trigram. Others, such as FID are known as CVC trigrams, the V standing for vowel.

One of the original methods of determining what a non-sense item 'means' for a subject is simply to ask him. Although this differs from the association method of assessing meaning-fulness the results obtained within the two procedures are closely related. Tables of norms exist for many CCC and CVC items and a useful summary of them is given by Kausler (1974).

Semantic generalization

Methods such as word association and semantic differential have a disadvantage when used to study meaning, for they rely on the honesty of the subject and are unable to provide a check on whether he is biased in his responding, i.e. un-willing to give some responses but very ready to give others because of what he fears the experimenter may infer about him from his responses. It is not easy to check if associative responses are spontaneous, or whether the number of respon-ses given in tests of meaningfulness represent all the items the subject is able to produce. Usually subjects give every indication of cooperating but where tests are employed for purposes of diagnosis in psychoanalytic techniques, for ex-ample, the lack of control over the patient's willingness to respond may be a distinct drawback. This point was made by two Russians, A. R. Luria and O. S. Vinogradova (1959), who proposed a more objective method for exploring seman-tic relations.

Luria's experiment. The technique involved what are known as *orienting reflexes*. If a subject is presented with a stimulus for the first time in an experiment then a reaction takes place in the nervous system controlling the blood vessels and this leads to a contraction of vessels in the fingers but a dilation of the vessels on the surface of the head. This reaction is known as the *orienting reflex* and it is possible to measure these changes in various ways including the amount of light passing through the body tissue of the finger; this varies as the rate of blood flow varies. An important feature of the orienting re-flex is that it gradually dies out if the stimulus is presented a

33

number of times, provided the subject does not have to respond to it. This dying away of the orienting reflex is known as *habituation*. If the subject is required to press a button when the stimulus appears then the orienting reflex continues to appear.

Luria's subjects were shown several neutral words which required no response and for which the orienting reflex habituated after repeated presentations. In addition they were required to press a button with their right hands when the word *koshka* (cat) appeared; the reflex was measured on their left hand. As expected the reflex to *koshka* did not habituate. The important finding occurred if a word related to *koshka* in meaning was presented, e.g. *mysh* (mouse), *sobaka* (dog); the orienting reflex occurred even though subjects did not mistakenly press the switch as required for *koshka*. The orienting reflex had *generalized* to words which were semantically similar to the critical word requiring the pressing response and it is necessary to explain how this occurred without the subjects erroneously pressing the switch. This is accounted for if identification of the stimulus involves analysis of the semantic features stored with the word in memory, because where the stimulus is semantically similar to the critical word they will share many of their features. Although the pressing response does not occur until the stimulus has been analysed sufficiently to enable a correct decision to be made, the nervous system may be 'alerted' by even small amounts of information which are characteristic of the critical stimulus. The technique therefore offers a way of mapping the semantic relationships of words by noting the extent of the orienting reflex.

Interestingly, words which sounded the same as *koshka* but had different meanings, e.g. *kroshka* (crumb), did not provoke the reflex, indicating that only semantic analysis of the words was permitted to influence the decision whether to press the switch or not. When children suffering from certain types of brain damage were tested it was found that similarity of sound rather than similarity of meaning provoked the reflex thus providing information about the effects of these types of damage on the analysis of verbal stimuli.

A further demonstration of the usefulness of this technique is given by the finding that when *skripka* (violin) was the critical word the reflex occurred to the names of other stringed instruments with the exception of harp, suggesting that logical taxonomic classification of the instruments as stringed is not necessarily the basis for subjective interpretation of a word's meaning. Possibly the shape of the instruments had something to do with what was considered similar.

Summary

Semantic memory contains words and their features which define them thus enabling it to fulfil the role of dictionary and encyclopaedia. According to this view it is necessary to distinguish between the word as a stimulus and the word as the collection of features which forms its representation in memory. The various methods of assessing meaning confirm that the relationships between word meanings are complex with large amounts of cross-referencing. The speed with which verbal items can be produced and comprehended in speech suggests efficient organization of storage and retrieval processes. The next chapter discusses the nature of such organization as revealed by the times taken to make decisions about word meaning.

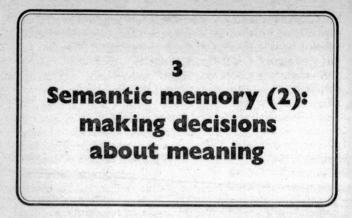

3
Semantic memory (2): making decisions about meaning

The ability to group things and events into classes or categories so that all members of one class can be treated as equivalent in certain ways is an important aspect of human behaviour. Solids form a category of substances distinct from liquids and gasses, and knowledge that a substance is a solid enables certain of its properties to be inferred. Thus knowledge that glass is a solid, despite its atypical transparency, will prevent someone from trying to walk through a glass door without first opening it! The categorization process is important because it simplifies a complex world by reducing the number of different types of things and events with which we have to deal; it reduces the information-processing load imposed on the organism. Categorization, the establishment of similarities, is the converse of discrimination, the establishment of differences between things and events. The use of language implies that categorization and discrimination must be possible when the verbal representations, rather than the actual things and events themselves, are involved, and semantic memory must contain sufficient information to permit these processes to take place. For example, subjects can correctly decide that the word *dog* refers to a type of *animal*, and that *tulip* does not refer to an *animal*. The biological definition of an animal contains the property that the organism must breathe, hence the decision that *dog* is an animal implies that a *dog* breathes. It is of interest to know if the lexical representation of *dog* has an *animal* feature and a *breathes* feature attached to it, i.e.

has a note allocated to it in the filing card model discussed on page 23, or whether the conclusion that a dog breathes is inferred from knowledge that it is an animal. The reasons for this interest will now be made clear.

A satisfactory model of semantic memory must account not only for the ability to make correct decisions of the type just referred to, but also for the speed with which they can be made. For example, the decision that a *dog* is an *animal* can be made in about 700 milliseconds and that includes the time to read the stimulus and execute the response, e.g. press a button indicating YES, (one millisecond = one-thousandth of a second). Also, the rate at which linguistic symbols can be interpreted and ideas translated into words during speech comprehension and production is about two words per second. Because of the large number of 'facts' held in semantic memory and the complexity of the relationships between word meanings these rates of interpretation and generation suggest that the input, storage and retrieval processes must be *economically organized*. Principles of economy in storage and retrieval systems are best explained by reference to computers which are constructed with such principles very much in consideration. It must be understood that it is not intended to imply that the human memory system works in the same way as a computer but, as was pointed out in Chapter 1, the use of things which we understand as models for things we do not understand can be helpful in developing our knowledge of the latter.

It happens that when the number of facts to be stored in a computer is relatively small it is economical to place them anywhere in the store and when one is required to examine all the stored items one by one until the desired fact is found. When large numbers of facts are stored this *serial search* procedure is uneconomical. Instead, ways have to be found to reduce the number of facts examined and this can be achieved if certain classes of facts are stored in one place (e.g. on one part of a magnetic tape, or one section of the computer's central store) and other classes stored elsewhere. This being done, then if the computer, taking the place of our subject for the moment, were required to decide whether or not a *chair* is an article of *furniture* it would only be necessary for a search of the *furniture* region of the store to be made. If *chair* is found in that region it follows that it is a member of the furniture category. In addition to reducing the time required to search for facts in memory this system has the advantage of being economical of storage space because it is no longer necessary for each word to have all its defining features stored with it as was suggested for the filing card model on page 23. It is not necessary to store a furniture feature with *chair* because this is indicated by storing *chair* with all other articles of furniture; it is only necessary to store with *chair* those features which distinguish it from other articles of furniture. This is essentially the basis of the semantic memory model proposed by Collins and Quillian (1969) which is now discussed.

Collins and Quillian's model

This model was developed from attempts to produce a computer program which could comprehend simple sentences. It is because of this background that the model, as it is applied to human semantic memory, has such a strong computer-science orientation. An incomplete portion of semantic memory is depicted in Figure 3.1 which shows the hierarchical structure envisaged by the model. Words are stored at different levels in the hierarchy with the location of each word signifying how it is categorized, e.g. *dog* appears under *mammals* because dogs have the characteristics which define mammals. Likewise, *mammals* and hence *dogs* appear under

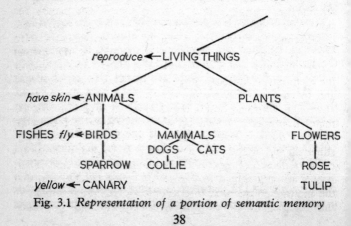

Fig. 3.1 *Representation of a portion of semantic memory*

38

the animal branch of the tree. In order to answer the question 'is a dog an animal?' the subject, as represented by the computer, has to determine that if the tree is followed upwards from *dog* it will lead to *animal*. It is assumed that progressing from one *node* (branching point) in the tree to another takes time, hence the more nodes which must be crossed to answer a question the longer will be the time taken to make a decision. In order to test the truth of the statement 'a collie is an animal' requires progression through the inferences 'a collie is a dog', 'a dog is a mammal', 'a mammal is an animal'. Thus three nodes are involved, whereas to test 'a collie is a dog' only involves one node. Collins and Quillian presented subjects with sentences of this form involving 0, 1 or 2 nodes (e.g. 'a canary is an S' where S is *canary, bird* and *animal* respectively) and required them to decide whether it is true or false. Of course a number of false sentences must be included to make the task real and these will be dealt with later on. The decisions were indicated by pushing one button for TRUE and another for FALSE as fast as possible but making as few errors as possible. The time from the presentation of the sentence to the pressing of the button was measured; the average times taken by all the subjects are shown in Figure 3.2. Clearly the time taken to confirm that the sentences are true increases directly with the number of nodes involved and the model is supported by this.

Subjects were also asked to decide the truth or falsity of sentences expressing property relations such as 'a canary has skin' rather than the categorical relations mentioned above. Collins and Quillian argued that it is more economical to store the properties common to all animals at the *animal* node rather than with each individual animal at the base of the hierarchy. Thus the property 'can fly' is stored with *bird* and to confirm 'sparrow can fly' involves progressing from *sparrow* to *bird* and examining the properties of *birds* for the required property. It can be see from Figure 3.1 that the effect on decision time of the level at which the property is stored should be the same as the effect of number of nodes on category decision times. This was found to be the case. Their results are also shown in Figure 3.2 and it can be seen that the increase in decision times per node is indeed similar to that obtained for the category decisions, although in general they take 200 milliseconds longer. A possible explanation of this difference is that it represents the time taken to search for the property at the node.

Although the model can account for the time taken to confirm true sentences several problems arise in explaining how false sentences are correctly rejected. The decision FALSE in response to 'collie is a flower' cannot easily be achieved by progressing up the network from *collie*, because presumably

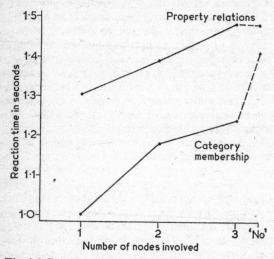

Fig. 3.2 *Reaction time for different types of question*
(based on Collins and Quillian, 1969)

the process must continue to the top of the hierarchy (*thing*, not shown in Figure 3.1) until the possibility of encountering *flower* is eliminated. This predicts that it should take much longer to reject a sentence as false than to decide it is true, and this happens (see Figure 3.2). It also predicts that it should take no longer to decide that 'a canary is a fish' is false than that 'a canary is a metal' is false but in fact the latter decision is faster than the former. The model has been modified so that 'journeys' through the semantic network from one node to another must be made either to determine which branch of the hierarchy the words are in, or to compare the properties stored with each word. Such modifications, however, still leave the prediction that faster decision times will occur for words which are close together rather than far apart in the network. Further modifications leave the model extremely complex thus eliminating much of its appeal.

Two major alternative explanations of the semantic decision data have been proposed. The first of these, the category-scan model, is principally concerned with category membership rather than property decisions, and basically proposes that the search through semantic memory progresses down the hierarchy instead of up it. In this way the statement 'a canary is a bird' is verified by searching through all the exemplars of the *bird* category and if *canary* is found amongst them the statement is true. The second alternative approach emphasizes the notion that the meanings of the words are compared for similarities and differences with decision times reflecting the decision-making aspects of the task rather than the structure of the storage system. We will consider these explanations now. The first model attempts to deal with the effects of category size on categorical decisions.

Category-size effects

Landauer and Freedman's study. Landauer and Freedman (1968) seated their subjects in front of a screen with each of their hands resting on a lever. The experimenter spoke a category name, e.g. *animal*, and two seconds later a 'target' word appeared on the screen. This target word could be an exemplar of the category, e.g. *collie*, or a non-exemplar, e.g. *cliff*. Subjects indicated their decisions YES, (the target is a member of the category), or NO, (it is not), by pulling the appropriate lever as rapidly as possible without making any mistakes. The time between the target onset and the response was recorded. The categories used were *word*, *noun*, *living thing*, *animal* and *dog*, the crucial feature of the experiment being that all exemplars of one category are also exemplars of the category on its left, e.g. all *dogs* are *animals*. In this way it is possible to conclude that one category is larger than another (has more exemplars) without knowing specifically how many exemplars are in them, e.g. all *dogs* are *animals*; not all *animals* are *dogs*; hence *animals* is a larger category than *dogs*. The task is somewhat similar to the categorization task used by Collins and Quillian and which was discussed earlier; the results are similar, also. These results showed:

a) For YES decisions: questions involving larger categories produced slightly longer decision times (540 milliseconds) than did questions involving small categories of a nested pair (530 milliseconds).

b) For NO decisions: decisions were again longer for larger categories (645 milliseconds) than for smaller categories (592 milliseconds) but this difference was greater than it was for the YES decisions.

Landauer and Freedman discussed three possible models for the categorization process and they are informative of the several approaches which have been taken by theorists both before and after they published their paper: we will examine these models in the light of their results.

Serial search model. If the representations of words in a category are stored together, then category membership could be determined for a particular word by searching through the words stored in the category. If the word is not a member then all the words must be examined before the correct decision, NO, can be made. In order to make the decision YES, however, it will only take a search through half the words, on average, before the target word is found because sometimes it will be found early in the search and sometimes later on. This means that if the category size is increased two-fold the time to search the whole category to make a NO response will also increase two-fold, but the time required to search through only half the category to make a YES response will increase by only half this amount. A simple example should make this clear. Suppose there are ten *dog* words and it takes ten milliseconds to examine each word in the search then it will take 100 milliseconds to search the whole *dog* category. (The decision time recorded by the experimenter will be longer than this because it includes the time to read the target word and make the response but this can be assumed to be constant whatever the size of the category). It will take only fifty milliseconds to examine half the words to respond YES. If there are twenty words in the *animal* category it will take 200 milliseconds to search all of them but only 100 milliseconds to search half. Now, the important thing to understand is the fact that the *increase* in time to search is twice as large for NO than for YES responses and this is true no matter how large the categories are or how much larger one is compared to the other. Since in Landauer and Freedman's experiment the average difference between large and small categories was only ten milliseconds for YES responses but fifty-two milliseconds for NO responses the serial search model does not fit the data.

Parallel search model. Suppose that all the words belonging to the category in question were examined simultaneously. The sort of mechanism required to do this need not concern us here because increasing the size of the category should have little effect on the decision times of either YES or NO responses. It may seem apparent that *no* increase in response time (RT) should occur but it can be shown that in practice small increases should occur with examinations taking place in parallel with each other, but they should be of the same magnitude for both types of response. Since the increase was greater for NO than for YES responses this model can be rejected.

Dictionary model. This model has already been mentioned (p. 23) when it was referred to as the filing card model. Basically the model proposes that words are stored in memory with the features which make up their meaning stored with them. In order to determine category membership the representation of the target word must be found and its features examined for the presence of those corresponding to the category in question. If Landauer and Freedman's results are to be explained in this way it is necessary for features concerning small categories to be found before those concerning large categories, i.e. the search must proceed from right to left across the filing card as shown in Figure 2.1. While this is not implausible it does not account for the effects of category size on NO decision times because all the features need examination before this decision can be made. If, for example, it takes longer to decide that *cliff* is not a *living thing* than to decide it is not a *mammal* then the system controlling the examination of the features must decide to stop looking for

43

mammal features earlier than for *living thing* features. Again, such an arrangement is not impossible to conceive but the model becomes very complex and ungainly.

Hierarchical model. Collins and Quillian (1970) claimed that their hierarchical model of semantic memory can explain the category-size effects found by Landauer and Freedman. This model, discussed earlier (p. 38), attributes the finding that the *collie-dog* decision is faster than the *collie-animal* decision to the different number of nodes separating the two words in the semantic hierarchy (see Figure 3.1) and not to differences in category-size itself. Landauer and Freedman had chosen their categories so that the smaller category was always *nested* under (contained within) the larger one: They had confounded the number of nodes involved in the question with the category-size, thus making it impossible to separate the effects of one from the effects of the other.

Collins and Quillian carried out two experiments to decide whether the number of nodes involved in the question or the number of exemplars contained in the category is the crucial factor. In the first experiment they compared the time taken to decide on membership of small and large categories which are *not* nested one inside the other, e.g. *dog* and *bird* (there are fewer types of dogs than of birds, and no animal can be a member of both categories). If Landauer and Freedman's results were due to category-size and not nesting of categories, then decision times should be related to category-size in this situation where nesting is not present. The results showed that the time to confirm category membership was not related to category-size, but when nested categories, e.g. *animals* and *dogs*, were used in the second experiment Landauer and Freedman's results were replicated. These two experiments of Collins and Quillian support their hierarchical model and suggest that what appears to be an effect of category-size is really due to the nesting of smaller categories within larger ones. Although several aspects of these experiments have been criticized the hierarchical model accounts for the findings obtained for questions to which the correct answer is YES. It has great difficulty, however, in explaining the finding (discussed already on p. 40) that it is more difficult to decide NO if the exemplar is closely related to the category, as with *tulip-dog* rather than *copper-dog*. This phenomenon has been largely responsible for a class of models which emphasize the comparison of word meanings rather than searches through a semantic *structure*. This class of models is now discussed.

Feature comparison models. This class of models proposes that when the verification of the statement 'a collie is a dog' is required the features representing the meanings of the two words are compared. If the features are similar, that is if they match each other to a greater rather than a lesser extent, the words are judged similar; if they do not match each other sufficiently the words are judged dissimilar. By way of illustration let us consider an experiment carried out by Schaeffer and Wallace (1970). They presented subjects with pairs of words such that each word was a tree, flower, bird or mammal (note that these categories fall into larger ones of plant or animal). Subjects were required to indicate as quickly as possible whether or not the exemplars were members of the same category. The times taken to make the decisions for 'different' pairs are of interest because the network model of Collins and Quillian, in its basic form, predicts that the semantically close pairs, i.e. close in the network, should require less journey time to get from one to the other and hence should be associated with faster decision times than distant pairs. Schaeffer and Wallace's results indicated quite clearly that the close pairs took longer than the distant pairs for decisions; semantic similarity made it difficult to arrive at DIFFERENT decisions. While the network model fails to account for these results the feature-comparison model does so by maintaining that when *oak-tulip* form the pair they possess similar sets of features; they are living things, grow, have leaves etc., and when the sets are compared the extent of the overlap will make a DIFFERENT decision difficult to arrive at. The greater the overlap in the feature sets of the two words the more difficult it is to say DIFFERENT but the easier it is to say SAME; the smaller the overlap the more difficult it is to say SAME but the easier to say DIFFERENT.

Summary

The chapter has discussed the use of reaction time procedures to explore the characteristics of semantic memory. The discussion has been limited to a narrow range of tasks involving decisions about the meanings of nouns, specifically decisions concerning property and categorical relations. One class of semantic memory models constructed to explain the experimental results makes the assumption that information is stored economically (see p. 37) and the length of time taken to make decisions increases with the number of stages which must be 'worked through' to gain access to the information in the memory store. Neither the network model of Collins and Quillian nor the category-search model of Landauer and Freedman can adequately explain the results. Schaeffer and Wallace's feature-comparison model emphasizes the decision-making aspects of the task, i.e. what is done with the information when it has been retrieved from memory. Any adequate explanation of this very limited range of semantic memory phenomena must depend on appropriate methods of separating the extent to which the retrieval and decision processes individually affect reaction times.

4
Imagery

Images are reconstructions of sensory experiences and are formed from information stored in memory. When we 'picture to ourselves' a friend's face, or 'hear in our imagination' a piece of music, it is necessary for the original experiences to have been stored in memory somehow and to be recovered when required. Imagery can occur in all the forms in which the original sensations were experienced: it is often possible to 'relive' a particular experience such as swimming in the sea, and to image the view of the beach, to 'hear' the roar of the surf, 'taste' the salt, 'feel' the water, and even image the sensations of muscular activity involved in swimming.

Under normal circumstances imagery can be readily separated from actual sensation, for the individual knows that the images are not the result of his perceiving an actual stimulus. The presence or absence of the stimulus forms the basis for distinguishing between sensation and imagery, the latter occurring in the absence of the stimulus to which the experience refers. Another difference, which the reader can verify for himself, is apparent when attempts are made to inspect images in detail, whereupon they tend to dissolve or fade. Sensations, by contrast, become more distinct with directed attention.

Imagery forms the basis of dreams and more often than not the dreamer, when awakened, remembers the dream as having the quality of reality. This is particularly so with nightmares although even here the individual realizes the true, dream nature of his experiences. In extreme cases imagery takes the form of hallucinations in which the person cannot distinguish imagery from reality with the result that his behaviour appears bizarre to an observer.

Chapters 2 and 3 explored the concept of *meaning* from its verbal aspect. It was pointed out then that this verbal aspect is only one of several aspects, as the imaginal 'responses' evoked by words also form an important part of their meaning. Words differ in the extent to which they evoke images just as they differ in the number of verbal associative responses they elicit. For example, a word representing a concrete object such as *house* may well evoke the image of a house as well as eliciting the verbal associate *roof*. Other words representing abstract concepts such as *justice* evoke visual images only indirectly and with difficulty although the verbal responses may be abundant and appear rapidly.

In the early 1900s imagery was largely rejected as the basis of memory despite the very strong subjective evidence that it is a commonly occurring phenomenon and plays an important part in aids to remembering as we will see in Chapter 8. There were several reasons why imagery fell from the dominant role in explaining remembering it had occupied since the time of the early Greeks, and it will be useful to consider some of them here. Before the end of the nineteenth century the method of *introspection* formed the basis of psychological investigation. Introspection is the method in which the subject, who was usually the investigator as well, attempts to observe and classify his thoughts and experiences while solving problems, learning, recalling or doing any other cognitive activity. In this way it was intended to explore the nature and functions of mental processes. At the turn of the century these traditional procedures were being questioned because investigations in which only one person can make observations are not generally acceptable as scientifically rigorous: the reports of the observer cannot be checked and so he is open to the criticism of bias and distortion, particularly if he happens to be investigator as well as subject, and is known to have an interest in establishing one theory rather than another. Imagery fell from favour with the dissatisfaction with introspection because images are not observable directly by anybody other than the person who is doing the imaging. Although recent developments in the measurement of eye movements and recording of electrical activity in the brain have made it possible to observe some aspects of what is going on when the subject reports imagery, the basic problem of the *private* nature of imagery remains.

Imagery as word-meaning

Concrete and abstract words

The image was recognized by early philosophers as an important aspect of word-meaning because they considered images to be the internal representation of things in the 'outside' world. The Associationists held that images come to form part of a word's meaning through the mechanism of association; the frequent occurrence of the 'word' (written or spoken) in close temporal proximity to the object, such as happens when naming the object, leads to the formation of an association between the two so that eventually the word comes to evoke the image, just as the object does during actual perception of it. Accordingly, words which refer to concrete objects, e.g. *table*, should readily evoke visual images of those objects. Words which refer to abstract concepts such as *truth* will not become directly associated with concrete objects and hence will not directly evoke images. Thus, concrete words, which refer directly to concrete objects, have images as part of their meaning in addition to the verbal responses discussed in Chapters 2 and 3. In contrast, the meanings of abstract words consist largely of verbal responses.

While abstract words do not evoke images directly they may do so indirectly. The stimulus word *law* may provoke the image of a policeman through the verbal associations between *law* and *policeman*. Similarly, verbs or adjectives can only evoke visual images through combination with concrete objects such as 'the *running* boy' or 'the *large* tree'. Images in other modalities may be evoked directly by adjectives such as *hot*.

Speed of image formation. Evidence that concrete words evoke images more directly than do abstract words was obtained in an experiment conducted by Allan Paivio (see Paivio, 1971, p. 64). He divided his subjects into two groups and instructed one group to form a verbal association in response to each of the stimulus words when they appeared, but instead of calling out the association they were instructed to press a key as soon as it was formed internally. The second group were instructed to form an image in response to the word and to press the button when they had managed to do so. Both groups were shown a sequence containing both concrete and abstract words and the times between presentation and the subjects' responses were recorded. It took longer to generate both images and verbal associations for abstract words compared to concrete words, but while it took about half a second longer to form a verbal association it took about $1\frac{1}{2}$ seconds longer to form an image. The results suggest that concrete words do evoke images more directly than abstract words, but in addition they elicit verbal associations more readily. Concrete words appear to have the benefit of richer meanings in both the verbal and imaginal aspects!

It can be objected that Paivio had no means of checking that subjects were carrying out his instructions and not pressing the button on some basis other than the formation of the desired internal 'response'. If this were so it is unlikely that the *differences* between reaction times for concrete and abstract words should vary when the type of response is changed.

Type of imaginal response. The nature of the image evoked by a stimulus word depends on the subject's experience of the word or the object it represents and his interpretation of the instructions given in an experimental situation. The image is usually not specific; it is not an image of a particular object but rather a *generic* representation or composite picture typical of the class of objects to which the word refers. Images of specific objects are formed if the instructions require it, e.g. 'form an image of *your* house', or if the object referred to has some special significance for the subject as would be the case if he had just bought a new house. In some ways the evoking of images in response to words is similar to the production of verbal associative responses in that the type of response depends on what the subject considers the rules of the task to be (see p. 30).

Measuring imagery values. The imagery value of a word

indicates how directly it gives rise to imagery and it is usually assessed by asking subjects to rate the ease with which they can form a corresponding image. The image need not be visual; it can be tactile, auditory etc.

Once again, the difficulty arises in determining just what the subject bases his rating on. Despite the fact that it is not possible to observe his imagery and compare his rating with it, the scaling procedure appears justified because the results form a coherent pattern when considered with other word-characteristics. For example, Paivio, Yuille and Madigan (1968) took 925 nouns and obtained three measures for each of them: The measures were (1) concreteness – abstract rating, c; the words were rated on a 7-point scale indicating *how directly* the words referred to things; (2) imagery rating, I; the words were rated on a 5-point scale indicating how readily they aroused an image; (3) meaningfulness, m; this was the usual measure of verbal associative meaning (see p. 28). The two measures c and I were found to be closely related, i.e. words which were high on one were nearly always high on the other. The reason why c and I are not *perfectly* related is because words like *anger* and *happiness* are abstract words, having no direct reference to things, but they do evoke images of experiences that may be described as 'emotional', and hence receive high I and low c ratings. Paivio points out that another atypical set of words are those which are rated higher on c than on I; although these words are known to refer to concrete objects the subject is unfamiliar with them and so cannot form an image. These words are exemplified by *antitoxin* and *armadillo*.

Interestingly, high imagery words also tend to be highly meaningful, that is, I and m are closely related. This implies that concrete words have more extensive verbal associative responses because these are added to by the imagery which concrete words evoke. This explanation fits in well with the position adopted by Paivio over many years, namely that abstract words have their meaning largely accounted for by verbal responses, while concrete words have *additionally* imaginal responses in their meanings. When we consider *mediation* in Chapter 8 we will see that the imagery evoked by concrete words gives them an advantage over abstract words in many memory tasks.

At the beginning of this chapter images were described as reconstructions of sensory experiences. It is not possible to keep strictly to this description in the light of the previous section in which it was revealed that some imaginal responses to words do not represent specific objects which the subject has seen but rather consist of a typical object in the class denoted by the word. It is possible to maintain, however, that images are *constructions* made from memories of many or few sensory experiences, depending on the contents of the image. In this section we will be concerned mainly with the ability to image specific objects, feelings etc. Images which are formed on the basis of information which has been held in memory for some time before being utilized, and which can be formed again at some later time, must be distinguished from *after-images*; these are relatively short-lived and once decayed cannot be reconstructed without further stimulation.

After-images

After-images occur in all modalities but it will be sufficient to discuss only the visual after-image to make the differences between these and *memory images* clear. After-images occur when the sensory effects of a stimulus persist after the stimulus is removed. *Positive* after-images are those in which the image has the same brightness and colour relations as the stimulus, i.e. the bright parts of the stimulus appear bright in the image and the colours remain the same. These positive images are most clearly produced by bright but brief stimuli and persist for only a few seconds. Two important features of after-images are (1) they move with the eyes, indicating that they are 'peripheral', being located at the periphery of the visual system on the retina; (2) they can be eliminated by another visual stimulus presented after the original. This *masking* effect can be used to study other properties of this peripheral memory store as described in Chapter 5.

The positive after-image fades rapidly and is replaced by a *negative* image so named because bright parts of the stimulus appear dark, and dark parts appear light. Also, colours are replaced by their complements, e.g. if the stimulus is red, the image is green; if the stimulus is blue, the image is yellow. These effects can be readily produced by staring fixedly at a small coloured square placed on a white surface. After steadily fixating the square for about thirty seconds remove it and stare at the white card; after a few seconds the negative after-image will appear. A surprising aspect of the after-image can be observed; if the white card is moved away from the eye the image will expand. It is as though the perceptual system is interpreting the retinal image as though it were simply arising from a real stimulus fixed to the card. This is not unreasonable since the stimulus would have to expand as it is moved away if it is to produce an image of constant size on the retina.

Both positive and negative after-images are explained by continued activity in the retinal cells. In the case of the positive image, this activity is identical to that arising from the presence of the stimulus. The negative image is due to the fatiguing or run-down of light-sensitive cells so that they no longer function when stimulated. This means that the original colour of the stimulus is not perceived and the complementary colour dominates perception. Once the after-images have faded they cannot be restored at a later time without further stimulation, unlike the memory image which can be reinstated on many occasions.

Memory images

Some of the most remarkable observations of imagery phenomena ever made were reported by a brain surgeon, Wilder Penfield (1958). He had decided to operate on a patient who suffered from epileptic fits and so had exposed the patient's brain. Before completing the surgery he stimulated the surface of the brain in various places with an electric current. When the *temporal lobes* on the sides of the brain were stimulated the patient, who was conscious, reported various forms of imagery depending on where the current was applied. The images ranged from flashes of light to music, and stimulation of one part of the temporal lobes produced memories which were identified as originating in childhood and containing both voices and visual scenes. Penfield believed that the stimulation led to the retrieval of memories which would never have been retrieved under normal circumstances. While

53

this is difficult to test (the subject *may* have recalled these events at some later date if he had not undergone the operation) Penfield's findings demonstrate the large amount of information stored away in the brain and which can be brought into 'awareness' given the necessary stimulus for retrieval.

Vividness of images. Individuals differ enormously in their ability to produce images. Francis Galton introduced the questionnaire method of assessing the vividness of imagery experienced by an individual and he reported an investigation which was used in his book *Statistics of Mental Imagery*, published in 1880. He asked 100 men to remember what they had for breakfast on the day of the test. He was interested in the vividness and clarity of any images in any modalities, i.e. seeing, smelling etc. The results showed a wide range in the ability to image and in the type of imagery which was dominant. About 90 per cent of all those reporting imagery indicated that visual imagery was the most vivid and clear, 5 per cent reported auditory imagery as dominant with kinaesthetic (muscular effort) imagery dominant for the remaining 5 per cent. More recent studies have confirmed these findings.

The questionnaire does not provide the objective test of imagery that scientific rigour ideally requires since the vividness rated by the subject cannot be measured by anyone else. A procedure originated by C. W. Perky in 1910 does have objectivity and could provide a means of assessing vividness. Perky asked subjects to look at a plain screen and image an object, e.g. a banana. Unknown to the subject the experimenter projected a photograph of the object on the screen, starting at a very low level of intensity and increasing it gradually. Under these circumstances it is difficult for many subjects to distinguish their own images from that projected by the experimenter, although they often express surprise that 'their' images are not where they expect them to be. It seems likely that a subject who is not able to produce visual imagery would be aware of the experimenter-produced stimulus earlier than subjects who could produce images.

Manipulation of imagery. Individuals differ in the extent to which they can voluntarily manipulate the images they experience. Several tests have been devised to measure the degree of control and these usually include questions of the form: Can you image your car? Can you now 'see' its colour? Questions of this sort establish the presence of images. To test the ability to manipulate, the following type of question is included: Can you now 'see' it in a different colour? Can you see it upside down? Can you 'see' it broken up for scrap? Some individuals are not able to manipulate their images and others have little control over them, as they change spontaneously.

There is evidence that manipulation of imagery can be used to improve athletic skills; Richardson (1969, pp. 56–9) summarizes some of the work done in this area. He points out that a high-jumper will often 'mentally rehearse' the physical actions involved in jumping and will 'see and feel' himself doing so. Other studies suggest that basket ball players can improve their shooting performance by using imagery for mental practice. One player was unable to make use of such practice because he could not control the ball which stuck to the floor.

In an objective study Shepard and Metzler (1971) looked at the manipulation of imagery in a problem-solving task. Subjects were shown line diagrams of solid objects seen from different angles. Each trial consisted of showing the subject a pair of drawings and requiring him to decide whether or not they were projections of the same object. Half the pairs required a YES response and half a NO, and the times taken to make the decisions were recorded. When the pairs contained the same object, the angle through which the object had been rotated to produce one projection, relative to the other, was varied. The important feature of the results is the direct increase in time taken to respond YES with the increase in the angle between the two projections. The experimenters concluded that the subjects had to rotate an image of one projection until it matched the other, and this rotation was carried out at a fixed rate, hence the direct increase in time with angle of rotation.

One other form of manipulation deserves mention. This is the ability to combine the images of familiar objects in novel ways. Examples of this are too obvious to justify much space here but the combination of an egg with human arms and legs to form Humpty Dumpty is typical. Undoubtedly much artistic creativity and the success of science fiction depend on this ability.

Eidetic imagery

The notion of 'photographic memory' is a popular one, doubtless because possession of such a facility would remove the effort involved in learning and the frustrations caused by forgetting. Some individuals, mainly children, do possess a facility which has a superficial appearance of photographic memory, but detailed investigation has shown such a description to be misleading. The facility, known as *eidetic imagery*, has characteristics which distinguish it from both after-images and memory images, as will be made clear now.

One of the most impressive studies of eidetic imagery was conducted by G. W. Allport at Cambridge in 1922, in which he tested sixty children aged about eleven years. He asked them to look carefully at a fairly complex coloured picture depicting a scene containing people, houses etc. and let them do so for thirty-five seconds. When the picture had been removed, the children were asked to look at a plain grey surface and to describe the picture. Half the children were able to give descriptions in remarkable detail; for example, some were able to read, letter by letter, the unfamiliar foreign word *Gartenwirthschaft* written on a building in the background, and to do so backwards as well as forwards! It was clear from the children's reports and from their performance that they were able to project a detailed image of the picture onto the grey surface and to inspect it as if it were the original stimulus.

Characteristics of eidetic images. Eidetic images have several characteristics which set them apart from both memory images and after-images. They last much longer than after-images and can be formed again after they have disappeared. A few individuals are able to recover a particular image repeatedly, even after a period of weeks. Unlike the after-image, the eidetic image can be scanned and the individual can inspect specific parts of it; but in contrast to the memory image, he can do so in detail. When the image is scanned, the subject's eyes move across the surface on which the image is projected and the impression that the image is 'outside' the subject is added to if the screen is bent – the image will often bend with it!

While eidetic images are very detailed it is not true that they are 'photographic'. They do not contain *all* the details of the original stimulus, some details or even whole sections of the image are missing or fade away and then return.

Incidence of eidetic imagery. There have been a number of studies of the incidence of eidetic imagery since Galton's work in 1880, referred to above (see Haber and Haber, 1964, for a recent study). There is general agreement that the phenomenon is more common in children than adults with something like 10 per cent of 11-year-olds having it but only 2 per cent of 14-year-olds. The incidence is higher among children with certain types of brain damage than among normal children suggesting that the phenomenon may be the result of abnormal brain functioning. This latter point does not, of course, suggest that possessors of eidetic imagery necessarily have brain damage!

Selection of the image. Individuals with the eidetic facility do not form images of everything they perceive. This is perhaps just as well because if a clear and detailed record of every experience were kept it seems likely that the memory system would become overloaded; there would not be enough storage space to hold all the records. It is appropriate to note that while Penfield's work (see p. 53) shows the existence of information in memory which is detailed and likely to remain unretrieved in normal conditions, there is no evidence to show that *all* experiences are stored permanently in memory. To return to the present issue, several researchers have reported that children who are able to produce eidetic images only do so when they are interested in the stimulus picture. Therefore the formation of eidetic images is not automatic but is under the control of the subject.

Summary

Three types of images have been discussed in this chapter: the after-images represent a fairly direct representation of the stimulus and are located at the periphery of the nervous system; eidetic images and memory images depend on the retrieval from memory of stored representations of sensory experiences. Memory images are common phenomena although the ability to form clear images and to manipulate the contents voluntarily differ between individuals. The level of voluntary control over imagery possessed by some people, and the variety of images which may be formed, demonstrate the amazing versatility of the human memory system. The role of imagery in remembering verbal materials is discussed in Chapter 8.

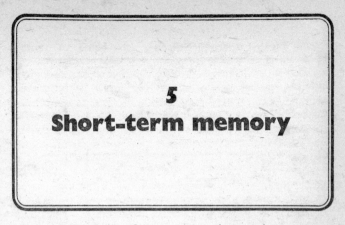

5
Short-term memory

Distinction between types of memories

In everyday life different sorts of demands are placed on our memory systems. We are constantly required to refer to our store of knowledge about the 'world' so that we may deal competently with things and events in it, and to semantic memory during the production and comprehension of language; in addition to these demands on the fairly permanent parts of memory there are short-term demands made by jobs which require us to remember information for a matter of seconds or minutes only. Examples of these short-term tasks include remembering a telephone number just long enough to dial it, remembering that we gave the cashier in the shop a £5 note and not a £1 note just long enough to ensure that we obtain the correct change, and a taxi driver remembering the address at which he must deliver his current passenger. Two important points about these situations require emphasis. First, it is not *items* which have to be learned; the digits, money, and street names and numbers are already in the participants' memory stores; what is crucial is the ability to remember that one address and not any other address known to the taxi driver is required by his current passenger. This distinction has led Endel Tulving to separate memory for the item from memory that the item occurred in a particular situation. He refers to these two aspects of memory as *semantic memory* and *episodic memory* respectively.

59

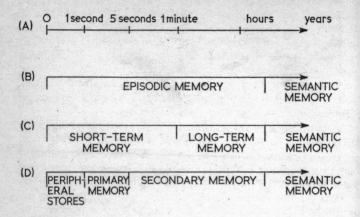

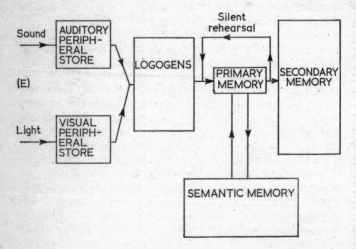

Fig. 5.1

The reader must be reminded here that semantic memory was distinguished from factual memory on page 12. Semantic memory was said to contain knowledge of the meanings of words and the rules for combining them into sentences. Chapters 2 and 3 dealt with semantic memory in this sense. Factual memory contains specific facts such as 'William defeated Harold in 1066'. Tulving (1972) appears to include under his heading of semantic memory both factual memory and semantic memory as defined here, but this does not cause any difficulty for the discussion which follows.

The second point to be emphasized is that it is often advantageous for information which is required for only a short period of time to be forgotten; if the taxi driver is unable to forget his last assigned address it will cause confusion when he tries to remember the current task. This last point suggests that an efficient memory system must enable the individual to remember some things for only a short period of time but to store other things for longer periods if he considers it necessary to do so.

Psychologists have studied episodic memory over retention intervals ranging from fractions of a second to years. This chapter and the next three chapters are concerned with these investigations although attention will be restricted to retention intervals up to about twenty-four hours with the main emphasis being even more specific – up to about fifteen minutes. One of the main problems arising when a student attempts to follow work on verbal memory is the different ways in which terms are used by various authors. Because of this it is necessary to clarify what is meant by some of the most important terms, and Figure 5.1 is intended to help in this.

Figure 5.1 presents a time scale at the top (A) which is not a linear scale. Line (B) represents episodic memory and semantic memory as distinguished above. Although the boundary between the two types of memory is shown as well defined there must be some degree of overlap between the two, i.e. there must be a region over which some episodes must persist in memory and become incorporated into semantic memory.

Short-term and long-term memory. This distinction, shown on line (C), is extremely vague. In a very fine review of this area Baddeley and Patterson (1971) suggest that *short-term* and *long-term* refer to the retention intervals used by the experimenter and not to specific memory mechanisms; we will see why in a moment. Because some experimenters have drawn the line between the two classes of intervals in various places, ranging from seconds to minutes, the classification as such is only of general use. Despite this several important differences do emerge between memory phenomena found with shorter, rather than longer intervals. For example, Baddeley (1966) found that information about words tends to be stored in terms of their sounds in short-term situations but in terms of their meanings in long-term situations. He found this by presenting his subjects with lists of words which all sounded alike or which all had similar meanings. After seeing the list the subjects were shown the words from the list in random order and they had to sort them into the order in which they had appeared in the list. It was more difficult to sort out the words which sounded alike when the sorting had to be done immediately the list had been presented, but when performance was tested after about fifteen minutes it was the semantically similar lists which were more difficult to order. Baddeley suggested that if acoustic similarity interferes with short-term retention it implies that items are stored mainly in terms of their acoustic properties; in long-term memory semantic properties are stored.

Memory stores. Line (D) of Figure 5.1 represents a view of memory which has been widely accepted for about ten years and which will be the main concern of this chapter. It must be emphasized from the start that alternative views exist backed by reliable evidence but the one depicted here accounts for a large proportion of the experimental findings and has the advantage of being relatively simple conceptually. According to this view information about episodes, e.g. occurrence of a word in a list, can be stored in one or more of three memory stores, peripheral, primary or secondary, depending on the retention intervals and other experimental conditions employed. Comparison of line (C) with line (D) shows that short-term memory performance can result from items being stored in, and retrieved from, any of these three stores, whereas long-term memory is assumed to involve retrieval from only secondary memory. The stores are represented by boxes in part (E) of Figure 5.1; the arrows represent the flow of information between these stores. The reasons for constructing the model in the way shown in the figure form the basis of this chapter and the figure should be referred to throughout.

Broadbent (1971) and Atkinson and Shiffrin (1968) have proposed models of memory along the general lines of the model depicted here and a fundamental aspect of this approach is that physical stimuli, in the form of light and sound, have to be converted into codes which the memory system can handle. Hence these models contain a series of coding stages in which information is held in one code while it is transformed into the code acceptable by the next stage. It is assumed that the storage of information in more durable form, i.e. passing it from left to right through the model, requires the expenditure of increasing amounts of 'cognitive effort'. This assumption has the backing of intuition, since we often 'have to make an effort to remember something', and of experimental evidence, some of which we will discuss shortly. The visual and auditory peripheral stores will be dealt with first.

Peripheral stores

If a stimulus appears for only a fraction of a second it is likely that it will have disappeared before it has been recognized and certainly before any attempt to remember it could be made. This situation is apparent when listening to speech when a rapid sequence of sound waves has to be integrated into phonemes and words: The beginning of a word must be integrated with the middle and end and this cannot be done unless there is some mechanism which holds on to auditory information long enough for this process to be completed. The situation is somewhat different for reading where the stimuli are present all the time but are fixated in a series of glances. If the stimuli fixated in these glances are to be comprehended they must be held in a store while the eyes are moving for the next glance. These considerations require that such stores have certain properties: first, they must take in information rapidly and this implies that it will be held in a fairly crude form since there will be little time to convert it into other codes; second, they must hold the information just long enough for it to be transformed into a more durable form, i.e. it must be cleared rapidly to make way for further incoming information. The stores are known as *peripheral* stores because they must exist at the periphery of the perceptual system, physically close to, if not actually part of, the sense organs themselves. They are shown in Figure 5.1 (E) to the left of a box labelled *logogens* which converts the signals given out by the peripheral stores into verbal form, by providing the location of words in the lexicon or dictionary of semantic memory (*logogen* is a combination of Greek words which mean *words* and *birth* and was devised by John Morton). It is clear from the figure that the peripheral stores are *pre-categorical*: they precede the transformation of the stimuli into verbal categories, i.e. words.

Iconic memory

The term iconic memory refers to the initially distinct but rapidly fading visual peripheral store. The basic investigations were carried out by Sperling (1960) using what was then a novel technique in which subjects are presented with a visual display of three rows of four letters each and lasting for up to half a second duration. If subjects are simply asked to report as many letters as possible from such displays they typically report four or five correctly (about 40 per cent). Sperling introduced the innovation of requiring subjects to report only one row of the display but they did not know which row until the display was switched off. The required row was indicated by a high, medium or low pitch tone sounded immediately the display ended. Subjects were usually able to report all the items from any of the rows and this indicated that all the items in the display are available for as long as it takes to transfer four letters to a more permanent store, but for no longer. That information in the store decays rapidly is supported by Sperling's finding that when the interval between termination of the display and onset of the tone is increased from 0 to half a second recall decreases accordingly.

There are several aspects of the data presented by Sperling and others which argue strongly that the *icon* or image held in iconic memory is a fairly direct representation of the physical stimulus rather than some verbally coded form.

First, there is the fact, mentioned above, that subjects can select any row on the basis of spatial location; second, items can be selected on the basis of size or colour; third, when letters and numbers appear together in the display in similar typeface no more letters can be recalled when cued for letters only than when cued for both letters and numbers. This implies that an item must be verbally coded to determine if it is a letter or number and this process takes up time from the life of the icon. Physical features form the basis for selection from the icon but verbal features do not; the icon is therefore pre-categorical.

Max Coltheart (1972) provides an excellent review of the work on iconic memory and suggests that items can be transferred to a more permanent visual store (not shown in Figure 5.1) at a rate of thirty milliseconds per item or coded verbally, via the logogens, at about 100 milliseconds per item.

Echoic memory

Echoic memory, the auditory equivalent of iconic memory, is rather more difficult to investigate because it is difficult to present materials simultaneously and cue for recall of only part of them. This means that techniques must be less direct in their approach than is the case with iconic memory. One recently developed technique involves comparison of serial recall scores for lists of digits presented visually or auditorily. In serial recall the subject must recall the items in the same sequence they were presented in. Curves A and V in Figure 5.2 show typical scores under auditory and visual presentation respectively, and represent the proportion of items from each serial position which are correctly recalled in that position. It can be seen that the auditory curve shows superior performance over the last few positions, and it is this effect which is considered to reflect the operation of a form of echoic memory known as *pre-categorical acoustic storage* (PAS for short) which holds acoustic information for only a few seconds.

It is proposed that PAS must hold two or three digits to account for the differences in the curves but it is not immediately apparent how it can do so because of what happens in the serial recall procedure. The subject must begin his recall at the beginning of the list so some time will have elapsed

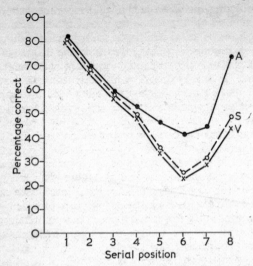

Fig. 5.2 *Serial position curves for Visual (V), Auditory (A) and Auditory with suffix (S) Conditions* (fictitious data)

between presentation of the last few items and their recall, certainly more than two or three seconds. To see how a store with a life of about three seconds can influence performance after a longer period we must look at a modified version of serial recall introduced by Robert Crowder of Yale University and John Morton of Cambridge. In their procedure lists of digits are presented auditorially but the last digit is always *zero* and this does not have to be recalled. The effect of adding this redundant *suffix* is dramatic as can be seen by comparing curve A in Figure 5.2 with curve S. It can be seen that the inclusion of the suffix lowers performance over the last few serial positions so the curve now looks similar to that arising from visual presentation (curve V).

The explanation of the suffix effect requires accepting the notion that PAS forms a temporary store in which auditory information is held for two or three seconds, just long enough to enable sounds to be integrated into verbal units by the logogens. The advantage enjoyed by auditory presentation compared to visual when no suffix is present is due to the fact that the last few items are held in PAS for some three seconds and have it all to themselves, since no further items enter it. The transfer of these last items to a more stable memory store is particularly effective, therefore. When the suffix follows immediately after the last to-be-remembered item it takes up 'room' in the PAS and so hampers the transfer of the final items producing a situation more like that for visual presentation for which the peripheral, iconic memory is very short-lived.

An excellent review of work concerned with PAS is provided by Morton (1970). This work includes findings that the suffix effect is greater if the list is presented to one ear and the suffix presented to same ear rather than to the other ear. This effect, taken with findings that the suffix may be excluded from PAS on the basis of physical features such as speaker's voice, suggests that the echoic store is indeed pre-categorical, being located towards the ear rather than further down the auditory perceptual system.

Primary memory and secondary memory

The evidence discussed in the last section supports the existence of peripheral stores in which information is held just long enough to permit it to be transformed into verbal units, and then cleared to make way for further incoming stimuli. Arguments similar to those made above can be put forward to support the need for a store which will hold the verbal code for a few seconds so that information about the items' occurrence can be set up in an even more permanent store if this is required. Evidence supporting the existence of two post-categorical stores is considered now, together with some of the functions and characteristics of the temporary store known as *primary memory* as distinct from the longer-term store, *secondary memory*. These terms, used initially by William James, were reintroduced by Waugh and Norman in an influential paper (1965). It must be realized that primary memory and secondary memory refer to parts of the memory system, unlike short-term memory and long-term memory which refer to experimental procedures (see p. 61). For the sake of brevity primary memory and secondary memory will be referred to as

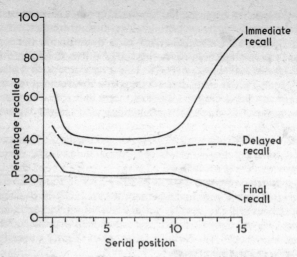

Fig. 5.3 *Free recall serial position curves* (fictitious data)

PM and SM respectively.

Some of the most convincing evidence for the distinction between PM and SM comes from manipulations within the free recall procedure in which subjects are free to recall the to-be-remembered words in any order they choose. When so instructed subjects generally recall the last few items in the list as soon as possible before recalling earlier items, provided recall takes place as soon as the list has been presented. Because of this these last items are recalled unusually well as shown by the *immediate recall* curve of Figure 5.3. This shows the percentage of words recalled from each serial position and represents typical results obtained from a number of subjects each tested on several different lists containing words which are not similar in sound or meaning to other words in the list. Of immediate interest is the superior recall of the last few items presented, known as the *recency effect*. It is obvious that these terminal items are retained in memory for a shorter time than other items because they are the last items presented but the first items recalled; there is less time for them to be forgotten. The evidence presented in the remainder of this section will be directed towards showing that the *recency effect* is best explained by accepting that items in the last serial positions are retrieved from PM and early items from SM rather than invoking the notion that there is only one post-categorical store in which information decays to give the serial position curve for immediate recall.

A clue to the explanation of the recency effect is given by the finding that it can be eliminated by delaying the recall. If as soon as the list has been presented the subjects are required to carry out a task which prevents rehearsal of the items, such as counting backwards rapidly by sevens from a given number, the serial position curve looks like the *delayed recall* curve of Figure 5.3. The early serial positions are affected very little by the delay but the recency effect is not now present. Since delay affects one portion of the curve and not the other it is reasonable to conclude that two separate processes are involved, one responsible for the recall of items presented recently and the other responsible for recall of earlier items. This explanation would receive convincing support if a variable could be found which affects the early part of the curve but not the recency part. Several such variables do exist including word fre-

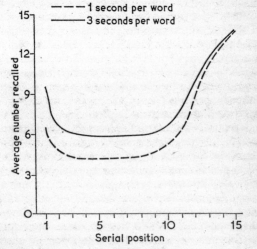

Fig. 5.4 *Serial position curves for different presentation rates* (fictitious data)

quency, meaningfulness, relations between items in the list and rate of presentation. By way of illustration, Figure 5.4 depicts typical curves obtained when subjects are required to free recall lists of fifteen unrelated words presented at either one second or three seconds per word.

The evidence presented so far supports the model shown in Figure 5.1 and in which PM has the properties of a temporary store in which items can be held long enough for additional processing to be completed. This function of PM and some of its characteristics are now discussed further.

Primary memory

Functions of PM. Murray Glanzer of New York is a strong advocate of the view that PM (what he calls short-term store) is a temporary holding device in the flow of information into SM. He also maintains that this flow to SM does not take place automatically; the subject has to carry out the right sort of activity to establish items in SM. This view seems reasonable if only because automatic transfer would lead to all manner of unwanted information collecting in memory. Glanzer has carried out several investigations which support this view. In one study (Glanzer and Meinzer, 1967) subjects were presented with lists of fifteen words at a rate of three seconds per word and required to free recall them immediately. In one condition subjects had to repeat each word six times before the next word appeared; in the other condition they were free to do whatever they wished. If the transfer of information about the words from PM to SM requires special effort then simply rehearsing the items will merely keep them in PM (see rehearsal loop in Fig. 5.1) and prevent the subject from 'working on them'. The results showed clearly that performance over the early, SM part of the lists was reduced by rehearsal relative to that for the condition where subjects were free to engage in any strategy they thought necessary to transfer information. The nature of these strategies forms the basis for Chapter 6 and consideration of them will be left until then.

The role played by PM in the establishment of more durable memory codes is emphasized by an ingenious experiment reported by Fergus Craik (1970). Subjects were given ten immediate free recall trials with different lists of fifteen words on each trial. When the proportion of items correctly recalled from each serial position was calculated the serial position curves were typical, i.e. like the *immediate recall* curve of Figure 5.3. When subjects had completed their ten trials and thought they had finished they were unexpectedly asked to recall as many words as possible from all the ten lists and to do so in any order. The words recalled on the *final* free recall were identified as to the serial position they occupied in the first part of the experiment. Thus, it was possible to assess the proportion of words originally presented in each serial position which were recalled in the *final* test. Craik's data is shown in idealized form as the *final recall* in Figure 5.3. Surprisingly, items which were recalled best of all on the initial free recall test are recalled least well on the final test! This result goes against common sense and trace strength models which predict that an item which is best remembered at one time will also be best remembered at a later time. However, such a view implies that the same 'memory' is being tested on both occasions; that is, the initial and final recalls are made from a *unitary* memory system. Craik's data can readily be explained if the initial free recall curve reflects outputs from *two* memory stores, the short-lived PM and longer-lived SM. If PM acts as a temporary store so that items may be processed for storage in SM then the terminal items in a list will have been in PM only a short time before they are 'emptied out' as the first items recalled. This means that the last items, having only just entered PM, will be easily recalled from it but the act of recalling them and other items will prevent the subject from processing them for storage in SM. Since the final free recall must be made from SM the terminal items will be least likely to be recalled, hence the difference between the initial and final recall curves.

Capacity of PM. We have assumed that PM is post-categorical; it stores verbal units, letters or words rather than sounds, as does PAS mentioned earlier. If this is true how many units can it hold and how large can each unit be? Before answering these questions it is necessary to consider the *methods* which have been employed to find the answers. Several such methods have been devised but space permits discussion of only two. A full account and critical analysis is given by Watkins (1974).

Comparison of the serial position curves for immediate and delayed recall (shown in Fig. 5.3) suggests that PM is influencing recall for up to about five items. This does not mean, however, that PM *holds* five items; it means that on most occasions the last item is recalled from PM (nearly 100 per cent correct), but only on a few occasions is the fifth item from the end recalled from PM. The comparison of the serial position curves does not give an estimate of the capacity of PM and other methods are required to do so.

In their influential paper Waugh and Norman (1965) proposed that establishing memory for an item in SM does not necessarily mean that it is removed from PM; items are not simply shunted about the memory system like railway wagons in sidings. This view implies that items constituting the recency part of serial position curves may have been retrieved from either PM *or* SM. Assuming that subjects can *retrieve* items from only one store at a time Waugh and Norman suggested that the probability of an item in serial position i (where i is any serial position) being recalled at all is given by the formula:

$$R_i = PM_i + SM_i - PM_i \times SM_i$$

where PM_i and SM_i are the probabilities that the item is retained in PM and SM respectively. This equation simply states that the probability of recalling the item is the probability that it is in PM *or* SM, the final term simply corrects for the assumption that if it is *in* both stores it can only be *retrieved* from one of them. A little rearranging of the formula leads to:

$$PM_i = \frac{R_i - SM_i}{1 - SM_i}$$

Since R_i in the formula is the observed probability of recall obtained in experimentation the important step in the calculation of PM capacity is the estimation of SM_i. Waugh and Norman suggested that the middle items in the list provide an estimate of SM performance and this can be used to estimate SM_i. Since this gives SM_i for all items in the list (for all values of i) and R_i is known for each item (given in the results of the experiment), it is possible to calculate PM_i for each item. The capacity of PM is then found by adding up the values of PM_i for all items in the list. This method yields estimates of capacity of about three items.

One severe criticism of the Waugh and Norman method is the assumption it makes that the contribution of SM to performance (SM_i) is equal for all serial positions. This is unlikely in the light of the shape of the serial position curve in final free recall (see p. 68) which suggests that the last items in the list have less opportunity, before recall, for coding in SM compared to earlier items. The value of SM_i should therefore be smaller for these terminal items. This means that the Waugh and Norman method probably underestimates the capacity of PM. An alternative, but similar, method is to use delayed recall to estimate the SM contribution to performance. Since PM is eliminated in delayed recall, performance must reflect only SM, and so enables SM_i to be obtained from the average recall of items in the whole list. This method has the disadvantage that performance is generally lower in delayed recall than in immediate recall and hence SM_i tends to be underestimated and PM capacity therefore overestimated. However, this method yields values of 2·1 to 3·2 items for PM capacity.

The capacity measure remains fairly constant whether the items are digits, letters or words and also remains unchanged when the word length is varied from one to four syllables suggesting that linguistic units rather than raw sounds are stored. This confirms placement of PM to the right of the logogens in Figure 5.1. The dramatic finding that PM capacity is 2·0 when *sentences* form the list items has been reported by Glanzer and Razel (1974). They presented subjects with a sequence of fifteen short sentences (about six words long) and required immediate or delayed recall after all the sentences had been presented. Each sentence corresponds to a word in the usual free recall procedure and the serial position curves were similar to those obtained with words as units. It is possible that subjects were storing the *kernels* or ideas of the sentences (see p. 22 on sentence production) and this implies that PM is capable of holding such units in addition to well-defined verbal units such as words.

Summary

The evidence discussed in this chapter supports the distinction between three classes of memory stores, peripheral stores, primary memory and secondary memory. The view which has been emphasized throughout is that the peripheral stores and PM are temporary repositories in which information about episodes (stimulus events) is held just long enough for it to be transformed into more durable memory codes. Because of the flexibility in the nature and size of units held in PM (digits, words, sentence kernels) some theorists have rejected the notion that PM is a 'box' of fixed size into which items are placed until transferred to SM. Rather they see it as equivalent to 'working memory' or 'consciousness' – what we are attending to. This view of PM permits the subject to fill it with, that is *attend to*, acoustic or visual features of words, their meanings, or even the kernels of sentences, depending on what he considers to be most appropriate for the task at hand. Clearly PM then becomes something more complicated than a simple box in which items queue up to be placed in SM; items can indeed be held in it for further processing and maintained in it by rehearsal, but names, meanings and even acoustic and visual images can be accommodated by it and these may be derived from external stimuli or retrieved from semantic memory and other stores of knowledge within the subject. These considerations have led to a recent reluctance to refer to 'primary memory' and to its replacement by terms such as 'working memory'.

The arrows joining primary memory and semantic memory in Figure 5.1 are intended to represent the fact that the subject can draw on his knowledge of word meanings and the relations between meanings of words in a to-be-remembered list to aid him in his task. Just how subjects go about utilizing semantic memory to facilitate episodic memory is the concern of Chapters 6 and 8.

6
Storage and retrieval

Everyone must be familiar with the experience of putting some object in a 'safe' place and then not being able to find it when required. The situation is made frustrating when there is a feeling of certainty about the general location of the object but the exact location cannot be recalled. Possibly a document concerned with car insurance cannot be found because the search takes place in the 'car' portion of the filing cabinet instead of the 'insurance' portion in which it was placed. Clearly the document is in the filing system but cannot be found because the rules used to store it are not being followed in the attempt to retrieve it. This analogy of the filing system is a good one for understanding one aspect of memory, the difference between storage and retrieval processes. The distinction between them is indicated by the common experience of attempting to learn someone's name and then not being able to recall it when confronted with the person again. It seems as though our memory adds insult to embarrassment when we are able to recall the name at a later date even though nobody has since told us what it is. The name was stored in memory but it could not be retrieved when required. The rules by which items or events are stored in memory are applied while they are held in primary memory, according to the model discussed in Chapter 5, with the subject utilizing whatever rule he considers best for the conditions under which he will have to do the remembering.

The processes carried out when subjects apply their storage rules may be conveniently divided into *elaboration coding* and *reduction coding*.

Elaboration coding. This form of coding involves addition to the stimulus code so that the final code is richer than the original. For example, if the subject is required to remember the sequence of letters T, M, I, W, F, A, W, B, T, R, he would find it very difficult if he simply tried to learn the sequence of letters as such, that is by what is generally known as *rote* learning. He would find it much easier if he elaborated the letters into words which form a grammatical sequence such as 'This Morning I Went For A Walk Beside The River'. It is likely that this elaboration of letters into words would be accompanied by visual imagery which would facilitate memory for the word sequence. Elaboration coding may be seen as reducing the uncertainty about the to-be-remembered items by embedding them in a form which has more certainty to it. Thus the sequence of letters contains no rules to help the subject; even if he recalls *T* it will not, on its own, help in recalling *M*. However, the application of the rule for converting letters to grammatical sequences of words reduces the memory load because the rules of grammar are already known to the subject. Given that he remembers the idea, or kernel of the sentence he can generate the words, and hence the letters, relatively easily.

Reduction coding. This form of coding involves a transformation of the to-be-remembered material into a reduced number of units which can be expanded again to give the original items. For example, if the task involves remembering a sequence of *ones* and *zeros* the subject can convert them into a smaller number of digits each representing a particular sequence. Thus, if we represent 000 as 0; 001 as 1; 010 as 2; 011 as 3; 100 as 4; 101 as 5; 110 as 6; 111 as 7, we can convert the sequence 001 011 110 111 into 1 3 6 7 thus having only four items to remember instead of twelve. At recall the four items can be converted back, provided the rule is remembered. Some readers will recognize this as converting binary digits (0 and 1) to octal digits (0 to 7) as opposed to decimal digits (0 to 9).

One of the interesting points to emerge from studies of short-term memory is the limit of about seven unrelated items which can be remembered. If reduction coding is employed such that three of the original items are reduced to one new item then about seven of the new items can be remembered. In a famous paper, Miller (1956) refers to the capacity of short-term memory as seven plus or minus two *chunks* (from five to nine chunks). *Chunks* are formed when the original items are recoded: Memory for seven chunks of octal digits will enable the subject to reproduce $7 \times 3 = 21$ binary digits. Some readers will remember London telephone numbers before all-digit numbers were introduced. The code for Euston was EUS and since subscribers knew the rule that the first three letters to dial were those of the exchange this represented only one chunk, and the whole number with its four digits thus represented five chunks. Now, the code for Euston is 387 and the seven digits represent seven chunks for those subscribers not familiar with the code.

The reason for introducing the types of coding employed in memory tasks was to present the notion that they represent the operation of storage rules which are utilized to retrieve the stored information at the time of testing. The remainder of this chapter is concerned with differentiating between storage and retrieval processes as well as their mutual dependence. To this end the discussion will centre on storage and retrieval rules falling under the heading of *organization,* and which are largely of the reduction type of coding. Elaboration coding will be dealt with in detail in Chapter 8.

Organization

The term *organization* refers to the relations between to-be-remembered items. Endel Tulving (1968), in an important article, distinguishes between two types of organization. *Primary organization* describes strategies based on relations such as position in the list, or grouping of items in space or time. For example, subjects are able to recall more random digits if they rehearse them in groups of three rather than attending to one at a time or trying to rehearse groups of four or more. Organization which involves the semantic aspects of items is termed *secondary organization* by Tulving. Secondary organization reveals itself in differences between the ordering of items in the presentation sequence and the subject's recall sequence as when, for instance, the words *big* and *large* are recalled one after the other even though they appeared widely separated in the presentation sequence. This reordering of items can only occur if the subject is able to choose his own recall sequence and hence studies on organization are restricted to *free* recall.

Secondary organization falls into two classes, that intentionally imposed by the experimenter and that extracted from the material by the subject even though the experimenter constructed what he considered to be a 'random' list with no semantic or phonemic similarities between items. The two most investigated types of experimenter-imposed organization are *categorical* and *associative*. The first of these refers to lists of to-be-remembered items which fall into a number of semantic categories such as *birds*, *metals* and *furniture*. The second refers to lists in which items belong to associative pairs or networks such as *hot-cold* or the *butterfly* network (see p. 32).

The study of organization and its effects on memory performance is of interest because it helps to answer questions about memory processes in general. First, it provides a means of determining some of the forms of coding employed by subjects; it is to be expected that semantic coding is prominent in secondary memory tasks (see p. 62) and if semantic memory is being utilized to facilitate episodic memory then categorical and associative features should be amongst those involved. Second, the effects of organization help to distinguish between storage and retrieval processes; it gives an indication whether organization is used to store information in some special way or whether subjects use knowledge of the list composition simply to narrow down the items in memory which could have come from the list. For example, knowledge that *animals* were present in the list will help *at recall* by focusing attention on animals rather than any other class of word, i.e. it reduces the uncertainty about the items to be recalled. This second issue is whether organization has its effect only at retrieval, at storage, or both. A third point arises from Miller's theory of chunking which is mentioned above. It seems possible that organization of the list into semantic categories, for example, will enable the subject to form a chunk with each category. If this is so, how large can the chunks be and how many chunks can be remembered?

Experimenter-imposed organization

Categorical organization. Experiments concerned with categorical organization are characterized by the selection of to-be-remembered words from taxonomic categories such as animals, first names, professions, and vegetables. The exemplars are then randomly arranged into the presentation list and shown to the subject with instructions to free recall. Bousfield (1953) initiated a series of experiments using such a procedure. He selected fifteen exemplars from the four categories just mentioned, presented them in random order, and requested free recall. The recall sequences contained clusters of items from the categories; first a group of animals might be recalled followed by a group of names, and so on; then possibly some more animals. Before any theoretical interpretation of the results could be made Bousfield had to determine how much clustering of items from the same category would take place by chance alone. One of the methods he used was simply to write each word recalled by a given subject on paper, put them in a box and draw them out at random. The amount by which items clustered together by chance was much smaller than that occurring in the subjects' recalls. Bousfield's explanation of clustering is not very straightforward but it is somewhat equivalent to the view that subjects remember the category names and simply generate exemplars accordingly. However they cannot do this in an uncontrolled way because there are usually very few intrusions (words given out by the subject which did not occur in the presentation list). This suggests that subjects are able to distinguish between category exemplars which did occur in the list from those which did not. There is an *editor* which withholds some category exemplars from being recalled and we will return to this point in the next chapter in which recognition and recall procedures are compared.

The similarity between the concept of categorical clustering and Miller's chunking is obvious; if each category acts as a chunk then there should be a limit on the number of categories recalled. But, how many words can be recalled from each category? Several studies show that for a list of given length, the number of words recalled increases with more, and hence smaller, categories up to about six and then decreases as the number of categories increases. With a list of twenty-four words recall is poor with one category of twenty-four words, increases up to four categories of six words and six categories of four words, and then decreases to twenty-four categories of one word each. Thus it appears that there are limits on both the number of categories that can be recalled and the number of words in each category which can be fitted into a category 'chunk'. This is made clear by the experiment of Tulving and Pearlstone (1966).

Tulving and Pearlstone presented lists of twelve, twenty-four or forty-eight words containing categories of one, two or four words in each. In this way they varied the number and size of the categories presented to different groups of subjects. Half the subjects were simply required to free recall the words but the other half were helped by supplying them with the category names at recall. As would be expected, subjects in the group who were *cued* with the category names recalled more words than the unaided group. Since both groups were treated in exactly the same way right up to the point of recall it can be concluded that they went about *storing* the words in similar ways; the difference in scores must have been due to the help given by the category names in *retrieving* the words from memory. The recalled words were sorted out into their categories and the numbers of categories from which at least one word was recalled were noted. Again, as would be expected, the cued group recalled from more categories than the unaided group but the two groups did *not* differ on the number of words recalled from each of those categories. The difference in overall recall scores for the two groups was due entirely to the fact that the unaided group retrieved fewer categories than the cued group. This point is made clear by the finding that when the unaided group were supplied with the names of categories not represented in the first recall attempt they were able to recall additional words from these categories to bring their total scores nearly to the level attained by the cued group. Tulving makes the point that the words which were retrieved only when the cue was supplied must have been stored in memory because they had not been presented again after the unaided recall; they were *available* in memory but not *accessible*. They became accessible when some help was given at retrieval.

A further important point emerges from this study in addition to the distinction between *availability* and *accessibility* of information in memory. If the cued and unaided groups are treated identically during presentation of the words, and if they also achieve the same number of words per category-recalled, then this measure seems to reflect the capacity of the memory system to code words for storage. If it takes 'cognitive effort' to form words into chunks then the time available during presentation will limit the amount of effort that can be expended and hence the size of the chunks. On the other hand, the number of categories retrieved by the unaided group reflects limitations on the capacity to retrieve from memory since the number of categories retrieved can be increased with help at the retrieval stage, i.e. at recall. Once again the distinction between storage and retrieval processes is emphasized.

Associative organization. Associative relations between words in a list are reflected in *associative clustering* in recall, again indicating that semantic relations are utilized in order to accomplish tests of episodic memory. Jenkins and his colleagues were the first to study associative clustering in detail. They constructed lists for free recall by selecting stimulus-response pairs from word association norms (see Ch. 2) and randomizing the order of presentation of all the items in the list so the pairs did not occur together. In one experiment (Jenkins and Russell, 1952) the pairs were always highly associated, such as *table-chair*, and twenty-four pairs formed the list. The average number of words recalled was twenty-four and half of these were recalled in associated pairs showing that associative organization was being utilized. In a later experiment the associative strengths of the pairs was varied. Pairs such as *table-chair* are said to have strong associative strength because most subjects respond with *chair* in response to *table*; *board* is not a common response to *table* so these two words have low associative strength. Lists were constructed in which all pairs had the same associative strength but this varied from high to low for different lists. Not only did the extent of associative clustering increase with increasing associative strength but so did the number of words recalled. This makes it possible to conclude that associative organization facilitates recall.

The method used by Russell and Jenkins for assessing the associative strength of pairs in the lists has some shortcomings, especially because it ignores the possibility that words in different pairs have associative strengths. To illustrate this, consider the pairs *loud-soft* and *piano-noise*; the pairwise measure ignores the associative strength between *loud* and *noise* and even if this relationship is not reflected in clustering, at recall, of *loud* and *noise* rather than of *loud* and *soft* it is possible that recalling the *loud-soft* pair may help in recalling *piano-noise*. This argument was expressed strongly by Deese whose work on associative networks was discussed in Chapter 2. Deese calculated an Index of Associative Strength which provides an indication of the associative strengths between all words in the list. It was found that the number of items recalled increases as the Index increases, and the two measures are more closely related than are recall and the pair-wise measure of associative strength. This suggests that subjects form chunks larger than the pair-wise units suggested by Jenkins and possibly make use of characteristics of the list as a whole to facilitate retrieval.

Recall performance is related to amount of associative organization but why does the latter occur? Does the subject make use of free association to generate the response item if he happens to recall the stimulus item of an associated pair, or does he have to code the words into chunks at the storage stage before associative relations can be beneficial? It is obviously possible for a subject to carry out the first of these strategies but the weight of evidence recently collected suggests that such a strategy is likely to be surprisingly unhelpful unless the rules were applied during storage, i.e. the latter strategy is the more effective. This issue will be taken up again in the section concerned with *retrieval cues*.

Approximations to English text. One form of organization

which may be imposed on the material is the extent to which the list of items approximates to the sequential properties of text. Approximation to text can vary from random sequences to perfectly legitimate sequences of prose. The important point here is that the predictability of the words in the sequence increases with level of approximation and this makes it easier to code them for storage and retrieval, e.g. it is easier to predict the next word in the sequence 'the man struck a match and lit the ....' than in the sequence 'struck and lit man the match the a .....'. As may be expected, the number of words recalled increases as the approximation to text increases, but this is due to the *size* of the chunks recalled and not the number of chunks; this remains fairly constant at 'seven plus or minus two'.

A form of chunking is evidenced when recall of sentences is required. Subjects appear to reduce the sentence to its meaning or kernel (see p. 22) which is retained in memory and then expanded into the full sentence at recall. Both sentence memory and the effects of approximation to English are dealt with more fully in A7 (Ch. 7).

Subjective organization
The phenomena of categorical and associative clustering indicate that experimenter-imposed organization provides a basis for the formation of chunks each consisting of several words. Neither categorical nor associative clustering is complete; not all the items in a category nor all the associatively-related items are recalled together. This suggests that the organization in the list as it is defined by the experimenter is not the same as the organization as the subject perceives and makes use of it in setting up his plans for storing and retrieving the words. Because of this, experimenter-imposed organization is not always the most revealing method for investigating how the subject codes the to-be-remembered items. Instead, what is needed is a means of assessing the organization utilized by the subject independent of any views the experimenter may have about the material. This is particularly true when investigating the recall of 'unrelated' lists, i.e. where the experimenter chooses the words so as to avoid the occurrence of relationships between words in the lists. It is not safe to conclude that subjects are not organizing the words

in the sense of forming chunks of similar words just because the experimenter has ruled out the most obvious kinds of similarity. If nonsense syllables can be elaborated into easily remembered forms then surely subjects can find and utilize relationships between words in the lists, given the extensive overlaps in word meanings revealed by studies of semantic memory. If it is accepted that lists of 'unrelated' words can be organized, the experimenter faces the problem of assessing where one chunk begins and ends; since the list has no organization as far as he is concerned, where is he to start looking for the similarity which forms the basis of the chunks? Let us look at an example just to make the problem clear. The experimenter may include in the list the words *table*, *cupboard* and *chair*, thus imposing the experimenter-defined organization based on the category of furniture. This will be revealed if the three words are recalled together. Suppose now that the words *table*, *ball*, *road*, *orange*, and *book* (which have no apparent basis for organization in the view of the experimenter) are included in the list and are recalled in the order: *road*, *book*, *table*, *ball*, *orange*. It seems that objects with flat surfaces are recalled together and then round objects cluster together, indicating that these classifications formed the basis of the chunks. In this case the grouping of words at recall appears obvious but this is not always so and in any case there is no way of knowing that the subject has not chunked the words into *road-book* (atlas of roads); *table-ball* (linked together by the game of table tennis) and *orange* (forming a chunk on its own). How is the subject's organization of the materials to be determined in such cases?

The problem of assessing the *subjective* basis of organization was resolved in a series of experiments conducted by Endel Tulving at Toronto University. He argued that if subjects are organizing the list items into *subjective units* then these will appear in the response sequence, but they cannot be identified because of the problems of identifying the beginning and end of each unit. If the subject is given a second presentation of the list (in a different order from the first presentation) and asked for a second recall, then his organization should be revealed by similarities between the first and second recall orders. Returning again to the example given in the previous paragraph, let the subject's second recall order be: *table, ball, road, book, orange*; this confirms that the flat object/round object classification was not used as the basis of *subjective organization;* rather, the *atlas, tennis, orange* chunks were used. In an experiment following the lines just described, Tulving (1962) showed that the number of words recalled from lists of 'unrelated' words increased over successive trials of presentation and recall, but so did the amount of subjective organization. This suggests that more words are recalled as chunks are more effectively formed. In a later study, Tulving showed that the number of subjective chunks stay fairly constant from trial to trial and increases in the number of words recalled from the list must be due to increases in the size of the chunks. There appears to be a limit on the number of chunks recalled (as Miller suggested) but the size of each chunk is increased as learning proceeds.

Part-list learning
Studies of organization show that subjects are engaged in chunking the list items into a reduced number of units which can be more easily retrieved than individual items because of the reduction in the number of units to be dealt with by the retrieval process. The theory of chunking emphasizes the way in which semantic memory is used to reduce to manageable proportions the load imposed on the subject by the task. Impressive though the theory is it leaves unanswered the question 'How are the chunks themselves retrieved?' One way in which this can be achieved is to incorporate the chunks themselves into a 'master plan' so that remembering the master plan will enable the chunks to be generated from it at recall. This notion fits in with the theme running through this chapter, namely that the rules to store to-be-remembered items must be re-applied at retrieval if the items are to be recalled. The matter cannot be allowed to rest there, however, because if this explanation of the retrieval of chunks is correct it should be possible to identify the nature of the master plan. The obvious candidate for such an identity is the general character of the list itself. That the *whole* list influences the choice of the master plan for retrieval is indicated by several findings, amongst them being Deese's demonstration (discussed on p. 82) that the associative relations of *all* items in the list with one another must be taken into account when

explaining recall. Other evidence favouring this view comes from experiments which show that learning part of a list before attempting to learn it all leads to slower learning than trying to learn the whole list from the start. Such findings are relevant here because if each word or each chunk were established in memory quite independently of other units, then if these can be recalled at one time they should be recalled equally well when other words are added to the list. If the units are not stored and retrieved in isolation from other units but are integrated into some overall plan, then the addition of new words may be expected to disrupt the effectiveness of the established retrieval plan. The effect of part-list learning, as the procedure is called, was investigated by Tulving (1966).

Tulving used two groups of subjects who were treated in an identical manner for the first part of the experiment in which they learned a list of eighteen unrelated words for free recall. In the second part of the experiment both groups were given twelve trials to learn and free recall a list of thirty-six words. Each subject in the control group received a list which contained *none* of the original eighteen words while each subject in the experimental group received the original eighteen words mixed up with eighteen new words. On the first attempt to recall the thirty-six-word list the experimental group recalled more words than the control group and this is hardly surprising since the experimental group had already learned half the words beforehand. On subsequent trials, however, the control group learned more rapidly than the experimental group so that by the fourth trial they were actually recalling more words. Tulving interpreted his results as indicating that the organization adopted to learn the original eighteen words made it difficult for the experimental group to fit the eighteen new words into it, or to adopt a new plan appropriate for all thirty-six words. The control group were able to begin organizing the thirty-six words unhampered by the previous, inappropriate organization.

Tulving's conclusions fit in with the view that if recall is to be successful the subject must set up rules for the coding of items during the storage phase of the experiment, and these rules must be followed at the time of recall. This view carries with it the implication that nothing can be remembered unless an attempt is made to do so and the view is embarrassed if learning does take place without any intention to remember the material. This issue is pursued in the next section.

Incidental learning

It is obvious that if the subject is to remember that a word was presented during an experiment *some* attention must have been paid to it; to take an extreme example, if a visual stimulus does not strike the retina of the eye then it cannot have an effect on the subject. If we are to study the differences in memory performance for items the subject intends to remember and those he does not intend to remember, he must be made to attend to the latter items but with intentions other than remembering them. Studies of incidental learning therefore tend to follow a general design in which one group of subjects, the *intentional* group, are told beforehand that they will be required to remember the material to be presented to them while the *incidental* group is asked to deal with the material in some way which ensures they have attended to it, but then unexpectedly they are asked for recall. Three points of interest arising from such procedures are: (1) is anything at all remembered if there is no intention to remember? (2) if so, then does the intentional group remember more than the incidental group? (3) do different orienting tasks directing the subjects' attention to the material in different ways lead to different levels of remembering?

There are several problems facing the experimenter in this type of research and they must be solved completely if the results are to have any value at all. Not least of the problems is that of convincing the subjects that the orienting task is all that will be required of them. Because of this they must not have obtained any details of the purpose of the experiment from subjects tested earlier. This problem is made acute for the experimenter who specializes in this field of research since word gets about as to the *real* nature of the tasks being employed. Despite all the precautions that can be taken there are still 'doubting Thomases'. For these reasons the orienting task in its own right must provide a credible purpose for conducting the experiment.

Recent research on incidental learning has accepted that it

is not possible to entirely eliminate the chance that subjects do attempt to remember items despite attempts to prevent them doing so. This acceptance is forced upon us by the need to demonstrate that no intention was indeed present before any learning which may be observed can be called truly incidental; it is not good enough merely to show that every effort was made to eliminate the possibility. Because of this the emphasis of research centres on the amount remembered under different types of orienting tasks rather than whether incidental learning is or is not possible.

It is possible to classify the orienting tasks generally used into two main types. The first of these requires the subject to pay attention to the physical characteristics of the stimuli such as orthographic and phonemic features, i.e. the subject may be asked to indicate whether each item has an 'e' or not in its spelling, or if it rhymes with 'ban'. The second type of task requires attention to semantic features and these may be placed in what may be considered order of increasing cognitive complexity. For example, it seems plausible that the decision whether the stimulus is a word or not involves less complex processing than deciding whether it is pleasant or unpleasant, or how frequently it is encountered in everyday conversation. Craik and Lockhart (1972) have labelled the degree of complexity of the orienting task as the *level of processing*, implying that some tasks require the use of information about the items which is stored deeper down in the semantic memory system than that required for other tasks.

James Jenkins of the University of Minnesota has carried out several studies in which he has varied the demands, i.e. the level of processing, of the orienting task and noted its effects on memory for the items attended to. In one of these studies (Hyde and Jenkins, 1973) subjects in the incidental group heard a list of words and as each one was presented they had to do one of four tasks; rate the word for pleasantness; rate how commonly used the word is in everyday language; decide about its part of speech, i.e. is it a noun?; and decide whether it contained the letters E or G, or neither. These tasks are ordered in what may be considered decreasing levels of processing. Unexpectedly, subjects were then asked to recall as many words as possible and it was found that the number recalled increased with the depth of processing involved in the incidental task. Also, the recall scores did not differ between the group making the pleasantness rating (assumed the deepest level of processing) and the intentional group. It follows from these results that, as the semantic component of the orienting task increases, its effects on the ability to recall words increases to the point where it is equal to that arising from intentional learning. How is this brought about?

It can be argued that subjects spend more time attending to words when the task requires deep levels of semantic processing compared to those requiring attention to the superficial, orthographic features. However, John Gardiner recently showed that this explanation does not hold because his subjects took longer to make orthographic decisions such as 'does the word contain a letter E?' than to make semantic decisions such as 'does the word represent a metal?'. Despite this, subjects making the semantic decisions recalled more words than those making orthographic decisions. Yet a further explanation, which does not have to resort to the levels of processing notion, arises from the possibility that the questions asked about the words provide cues for recalling the words. To understand the implications of this for the situations we have been considering let one group of subjects make semantic decisions of the form 'is it a wild animal?', while another group have to decide 'does it contain an E in its spelling?'. If the first group remember that some of the words were indeed wild animals then they will derive much more help in recall than the other group who have only the clue that some words contain an E. This situation may be expressed as one in which the cues available to the semantic decision group are *more specific* than those available to the orthographic group and hence more beneficial at recall (there are fewer wild animals than there are words containing E). This does not constitute an explanation of the effects of different orienting tasks because experimenters usually use a different cue for each word. In any case it is difficult to see how such differences in cue specificity can arise when the words are *all* rated for pleasantness or frequency-of-use, as in the Jenkins study; knowledge that pleasantness was involved does not narrow down the field of permissible responses.

The discussion of possible mechanisms underlying the effect of the level of processing demanded by the orienting task has brought us no nearer to understanding what is producing the effect. As it stands the level of processing notion is no more than a description, rather than an explanation. Perhaps we are more likely to find an explanation if we ask 'what happens to the word in the *intentional* situation?' Two points about the intentional learning situation have been emphasized throughout this book: First, *words* are not learned during a memory experiment; they already exist in memory and are operated on in some way to record their occurrence in a particular episode; second, subjects utilize semantic memory to facilitate episodic memory as discussed under the heading of Organization. What is clear from the incidental learning studies is that performance approaches that of intentional learning as the type of activity demanded by the orienting task becomes more similar to the activity which is assumed to give rise to organizational phenomena in intentional learning. Just how the subjects in the incidental condition go about retrieving words from memory when suddenly required to do so and having set up no plan at the time of storage is still rather a mystery.

Although we are unable to pursue the issue of how retrieval of list items is achieved in incidental learning we will return to the study of retrieval in conditions where the subjects are expecting to be tested for recall of the list items.

Retrieval cues

Organizational processes are directed towards setting up plans to facilitate the retrieval of information from memory; if an item is coded as a member of a chunk then it can be readily retrieved provided the chunk is retrieved. When none of the items in a chunk are retrieved, supplying the chunk label, e.g. the name of the category from which the items are drawn, leads to recall of a large proportion of them. This led Tulving and Pearlstone to draw their distinction between availability and accessibility (see p. 80): items can be available in memory but access to them cannot always be gained. The *cues* make the items accessible. One feature of Tulving and Pearlstone's experiment not mentioned earlier is important now. The words were presented to the subjects so that all those from one category appeared in succession, preceded by the category name; then followed the next category, and so on.

This has the effect of making it highly likely that each word is coded as a member of the designated category and in no other way, e.g. if *bed* is preceded by *furniture* as a category name it will be coded differently compared to its being preceded by *gardening*. Tulving argued that the cues were effective in bringing about retrieval because they supplied the plan by which they had been stored. However, the experiment they carried out does not provide a rigorous test of this theory because it did not contain a condition in which the category names were present at *recall* but absent during *presentation* of the list. It is possible that provision of the cue at retrieval will facilitate recall even if subjects had not formed a chunk out of each category; they may have simply worked their way through the exemplars of the category and responded with words which they *recognized* as being in the list. The distinction between these two possibilities is important: Tulving claims that the cue is effective in retrieving the words only if the words have been stored according to a plan which embodies the cue; the alternative view is that the cue simply directs the subject to consider a small subset of words in memory, e.g. *birds*, and it matters not what plans were used to store the list items.

Tulving performed two experiments to test the conditions under which retrieval cues are effective in aiding recall. In the first of these, conducted with Shirley Osler (Tulving and Osler, 1968) subjects were run under a total of sixteen conditions but discussion will be restricted to four which adequately demonstrate the essential point. The task was to remember twenty-four unrelated words presented one at a time and printed in capital letters. One group of subjects were also given an additional word printed above each to-be-remembered word in small letters. Subjects did not have to remember this additional word but were told it may be of some help in remembering the required word. These additional words which were to serve as cues at recall were all weakly associated with the word to be remembered, e.g. if MUTTON was the critical word, the cue word could be *fat*. The second group of subjects were given no cue words during presentation of the list. At recall, subjects in the first group who had cues at presentation, were divided into three sub-groups and either given the cues at recall to help them, given no cues at recall, or given cues which were different from the original, e.g. instead of *fat* for MUTTON, *leg* was given (also a weak associate of MUTTON). The second group, given no cues at presentation, were either given no cues at recall, or given the cues used with the other group. In essence, subjects had either similar conditions of cueing at presentation and recall, or different conditions of cueing. Table 6.1 gives the average number of words recalled under each condition.

Table 6.1

		Cue given at presentation?		
Cue given at recall?		NO	YES	
	NO	10.62	8.72	
	YES	8.52	14.93	(same cue)
			7.45	(different cue)

Data taken from Tulving and Osler (1968)

These results show clearly that cues are only effective if they are present at both input and output phases of the task. Indeed, provision of the cue under only input *or* output is detrimental because recall under these conditions is worse than when no cues at all are given. The lowest performances of all groups occurs when the cue is present at recall and (a) is different from that given at presentation, or (b) no cue is given at presentation but a cue is given at recall. This strongly dispels the notion that cues act only at retrieval. It is necessary for the same plan to be executed at retrieval as was used at storage if items are to be retrieved effectively.

The conclusion that to be effective, cues must be present at both storage and retrieval, has to be considered in the light of a later experiment conducted by Tulving and his colleague R. Thomson. The design was similar to the last experiment but the cues, when present, were either strong or weak associates of the to-be-remembered word, e.g. BLACK was cued with *white* (a strong associate) or with train (a weak associate), or not cued at all. Again, performance was highest when the conditions prevailing at presentation were repeated at recall, with the exception that when no cue was given at presentation and a strong associate was given at recall, performance was very high. Two possible interpretations follow. First, the strong associate is capable of cueing recall by the process of free association – this is the pure-retrieval explanation rejected by Tulving and Osler, which cannot be maintained because performance is poor when a weak associate is given at input and a strong one at retrieval. The pure-retrieval explanation must predict that the strong cue will be equally and highly effective when given at recall no matter what happened at the presentation stage. The second explanation involves the assumption that when no cue is given at input the item is coded in a way that implicitly involves the strong cue. If BLACK is presented alone then coding it in terms of its semantic features will involve the features possessed by *white*, the strong cue, because white is the antonym of black (antonyms possess the same features but these have opposite signs; see p. 30). The explanation preserves Tulving's position that cues must be present at both input and output to be effective, because it can be held that strong associates are suggested to the subject by the to-be-remembered words when they are coded, if they are not actually supplied by the experimenter; or, the features of the strong associates shared with the to-be-remembered words are coded with them at presentation.

Summary

Tulving's experiments have produced substantial evidence supporting his view, and the view adopted in this book, that retrieval of information from memory proceeds most effectively if the same plan is used to seek it out as was used to store it. The plans can be constructed by use of either elaboration or reduction coding. Those considered in detail in this chapter make use of semantic features to code the list items into a reduced number of chunks. Successful cued-recall of items from a chunk which could not be recalled without the cue force a distinction to be made between availability and accessibility of information.

The next chapter deals with recognition and recall procedures and what comparison of performances under both reveals about storage and retrieval. We will return to coding, that is, elaboration coding, in detail in Chapter 8.

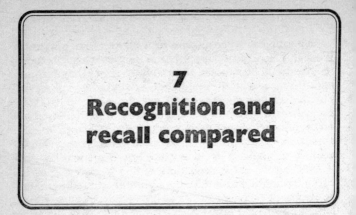

7
Recognition and recall compared

In a recognition test the subject is shown a list of items and then presented with these *old* items mixed up with some *new* items which had not appeared in the list. The subject has to decide whether each item is *old* or *new*. The essential difference between recognition and recall lies in what the subject must retrieve from memory storage to perform the task. In recall he must first retrieve an item and then, presumably, decide whether it is an item which did occur in the list before responding to it; in recognition he is given the item and so has only to retrieve information about its occurrence in the list. This suggests that recognition is an easier task than recall. It can be expected, therefore, that recognition performance is superior to recall, and items which cannot be recalled may well be recognized. It will be remembered that successful cued-recall of an item which could not otherwise be recalled indicates that the item is available in memory but not accessible; the failure to recall is due to failure to retrieve the item, not to failure to store it. The recognition test is rather like cueing recall with the to-be-remembered item itself, and because of this, comparison of recognition and recall performances provides evidence about storage and retrieval processes (particularly the latter) in a way similar to comparison of cued and non-cued recall. This type of research is directed towards answering such questions as 'what information must be retrieved to accomplish correct recognition, and how does this differ from the information necessary for recall?'; 'how is the information retrieved and how does the subject make use of it?'.

It is a common experience that it is easier to recognize than to recall. This is especially apparent in the case of memory for faces where a face can be readily recognized as familiar although drawing it or even describing it may be impossible. Witnesses of crimes are usually able to recall little of the criminal's facial features but can often pick them out on an identity parade or from photographs. The police endeavour to make use of the ability to recognize rather than recall in building up pictures of faces from components which the subject recognizes. The capacity of the human subject to recognize pictures is remarkable. R. N. Haber in America has shown that something like 90 per cent of over 2500 scenes of the sort bought by tourists could be recognized as having been shown to the subjects during experiments. Although recall was not tested it would almost certainly have been very low whether tested by drawing or description.

The general impression that recall is more difficult than recognition is supported by the findings of a large number of experiments in which one group of subjects is presented with a list of items and instructed to learn them for free recall, while a second group, given the same items, is told they will be given a recognition test. The recognition test can be conducted in several ways. If a single-item test is employed the list items are mixed up with new items and presented one at a time in random order, the subject being required to indicate whether each item is an *old* item which appeared in the list, or a *new* item which did not appear. In a forced-choice test each *old* item is presented with one or more *new* items and the subjects have to indicate which of these several items is the *old* one. The outcome of such experiments is that more items are correctly recognized as being *old* than are recalled, and this is true over a range of retention intervals from immediate tests to periods of a week or more. Indeed, recognition performance falls much more slowly than does recall, so the superiority of recognition increases as the retention interval becomes longer.

Threshold model. The trace-strength model of memory maintains that when an item is attended to with the intention of
remembering it, a trace is formed which has a high strength
to start with but which falls over time. It must be apparent
that this model does no more than describe memory performance; it does not explain it! Nevertheless, attempts have
been made to use this model to explain the superior performance of recognition compared to recall by combining it with
the notion of *response threshold*. According to this explanation
the strength of a trace may be too low to permit it to be recalled but still high enough to permit it to be recognized.

In order to understand the response threshold explanation
consider a situation in which the subject is shown a word
printed on a page but under very poor lighting conditions. If
the level of illumination is very low the subject will not be able
to report anything about the word. Under slightly higher
levels of illumination he may still be unable to identify the
word but able to decide whether it is a particular word or
not, e.g. if the experimenter asks 'is the word RUBBER?'
then the subject will most likely respond YES if he is able to
perceive that the first letter is R and the fifth letter is E. Perceiving this amount about the stimulus would probably be
inadequate to identify the word given no indication at all about
what it may be. This is similar to what the trace strength
theory proposes to happen in recall and recognition. The level
of trace strength, i.e. illumination in our example, may be sufficient to enable the item to be recognized but not recalled;
the threshold for recall is higher than the threshold for recognition. Figure 7.1 shows how this model explains the finding
that recall performance falls more rapidly than recognition
performance with increasing retention interval. The trace
strengths of three words A, B, and C are shown after retention
intervals of ten seconds and ten minutes. After ten seconds
A and B have strengths which are higher than both recall and
recognition thresholds and so can be recalled and recognized.
The strength of C exceeds the recognition threshold but not
the recall threshold and so can be recognized but not recalled.
After ten minutes the traces have fallen in strength so that
none can be recalled but all three can still be recognized.

Although the threshold model accounts for findings of superior recognition compared to recall it has some serious shortcomings which have led to its rejection by most theorists. The first objection arises because it predicts that recall cannot be superior to recognition. We will see later in this chapter that recall can indeed be superior to recognition if the right conditions are arranged! Second, the model predicts that if a group of words, say commonly used words, are easier to *recall* than another group, say uncommon words, then the uncommon words cannot be easier to recognize than the common

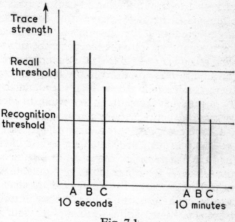

Fig. 7.1

words; they may be equally well-recognized but performance cannot be superior for the uncommon words. This can be seen from Figure 7.1 if B is a common word and C an uncommon word. Since it is easy to show that lists of common words give better recall scores but inferior recognition scores compared to lists of uncommon words, the threshold theory must be rejected.

Number of alternative choices. The forced-choice recognition test (see p. 95) becomes more difficult as the number of *new* items presented with each *old* item increases; performance, as measured by the number of *old* items the subject recognizes, falls as the number of alternatives from which he has to choose increases. Of course, with a choice of only two items, one of which must be *old*, the subject has a 50 per cent chance of being correct if he is merely guessing, i.e. has remembered nothing at all about the items in the list. (The same is true of the single-item test where an *old* or *new* decision is required for each item in turn.) As the number of alternatives increases so the likelihood that the subject will correctly guess which one is *old* decreases. This situation offers an explanation of the superiority of recognition over recall.

In recognition tests the number of alternatives is usually small, perhaps up to five in the forced-choice situation, but in recall the number of items to choose from for responses can be very large. If the list to be remembered contains unrelated words chosen at random from the language, the subject, asked for recall and receiving no help from the experimenter, is faced with the possibility that any word in the language could have been in the list. If he remembered nothing about the list the probability of guessing correctly is almost nil. In recognition, the choice may be between only a few words and in consequence, if he remembered only a minimal amount about the *old* item, it may be sufficient to enable a correct choice to be made. When the list items are drawn from a large set, recall is at a gross disadvantage compared to recognition. When the set from which items are drawn is small there should be no advantage to recognition because the subject can simply turn the recall task into a recognition task by generating all the alternatives and deciding about them one by one. This has been shown to be what happens in several experiments including that of Davis, Sutherland and Judd (1961).

Davis and his colleagues included in their study an experiment in which subjects were presented with fifteen two-digit numbers to learn. One group had to recall these numbers while the other group had to recognize them when mixed with fifteen, forty-five or seventy-five other two-digit numbers. Recognition was 63 per cent correct when fifteen *distractor* items were used, but only 40 per cent with seventy-five distractors. Recall, however, was about 45 per cent. It is clear that recognition performance is better with fewer alternatives but the important point is that since there are ninety two-digit numbers to choose from in recall, and these are known to the subjects, the numbers of alternatives are the same in recall and the ninety-alternative (fifteen *old* and seventy-five *new*) recognition test. Recall performance was actually slightly better than recognition in this last condition! Davis, who expected equally good performance when the number of alternatives were equated, explained the superior recall by the fact that subjects in that condition were able to recall in any order they found best; the recognition subjects, however, had to respond to the *old* and *new* items in the order determined by the experimenter.

The two-process model of recall. In the single-item recognition task the subject is presented with an item and required to decide whether it appeared in the experimental list or not. The word is presented and there is no doubt about which one the trial is concerned with. Some theorists have assumed that perception of the word, e.g. *cat*, as a test item automatically directs the retrieval system to the information which was stored in memory when *cat* was presented in the experimental list. In Tulving's terms, the information is directly accessible. Just what this information is upon which the subject's decision is made is unclear. Very often subjects merely report that *old* items 'seemed familiar'. Of course, some *old* items are not recognized as being *old* and this is explained by failure to attend to these items at presentation, or by the fact that as time passes items which were initially familiar seem less familiar. The other sort of error which occurs is that in which *new* items are called *old*; these errors are known as *false positives*. It is interesting that *new* items are called *old* more readily if they are commonly used words in everyday communication than if rarely used. This suggests that the familiarity of common words is high before the experiment and is mistaken by the subject for familiarity arising from occurrence in the experiment. Just what forms the basis of familiarity is not at all clear; some theorists simply utilize the concept of *trace strength*, with high strength indicating a recent presentation. Others suggest that associations are formed between the word and the general context provided by the list and the conditions in which it is presented. If, given the word at test, the links between it and the list are strong then it is most likely a list member. This may explain why *new* items which are semantically related to *old* items in the list are often mistaken as having occurred in the list, e.g. if *cat* is presented in the list, then *dog* stands a good chance of being mistaken as an *old* item. The semantic overlap between the two items leads to confusion in deciding whether or not *dog* belongs to the list, presumably because many of the features of *cat* which are coded at presentation are commond to *dog*.

In recall the subject has a different starting point to his task. We saw in Chapter 6 that subjects organize the list items into a plan which forms the starting point for retrieval. The objective in recall is to retrieve the list items themselves rather than starting with these items and deciding if they are associated with the plan of the list. Recall appears to require that items are *searched* for in memory with the retrieval plan to guide the search. In this way, with a categorized list, the subjects will direct the search to members of the specified categories. However, a notable feature of recall is the very small number of intrusions which occur (responses which did not appear in the list). These intrusions, when they do occur, are similar to false positives in recognition in that they reflect the acceptance by the subject that the word was in the list when it was not. Presumably other words are retrieved from memory but not given as responses because the subject is able to decide that they did not appear in the list. These considerations have led to the view that recall consists of two processes, a *search* process in which items are retrieved from memory, and a *decision* process in which these items are recognized as list members and given as responses, or rejected and not given as responses. According to this view, the decision process is equivalent to a recognition test; the item is now 'present' and the subject can make his acceptance or rejection in the ways described above for recognition tests.

The two-process model of recall has several advantages, one of which is that it provides an explanation of the finding that commonly-used words are easier to recall but more difficult to recognize than uncommon words. The threshold model cannot handle this state of affairs, as noted above. The two-process model accounts for these findings by maintaining that the familiarity of uncommon words is relatively easy to assess because an additional occurrence in the experiment is easy to detect amongst a background of few pre-experimental occurrences rather than the many such occurrences of common words; uncommon words should therefore be easy to recognize. Common words, on the other hand, tend to be concrete, to have extensive associative networks and generally to possess properties which facilitate organization and hence retrieval. In recall, then, more common words should be retrieved, but because recognition is poor relative to uncommon words there should be more intrusions. This does indeed occur. Other, more complex, explanations of the effects of the frequency of everyday use on recognition and recall are possible but space does not permit further elaboration.

The two-process model of recall accounts for findings that recognition is superior to recall (when both tests involve the same items) by the presence of the additional stage in recall. There are two processes which must function correctly if recall is to be successful, but only one in recognition. Importantly, if the search process fails in recall it is possible that the subject could recognize the item if given to him. This happens and suggests that the information about the item is available in memory but not accessible under the cues provided in recall. When the item itself is provided as a cue then access can be gained to the necessary information.

When recall is better than recognition. The two-process model of recall implies that recall cannot be superior to recognition because any failure in the decision process should affect both tests but recall is additionally dependent on the search process. This position is challenged by Tulving who conducted a surprisingly simple test for it. Tulving's subjects were first of all required to learn forty-eight pairs of words so that when presented with the first word of the pair they could recall the second word. The pairs were formed from highly associated words such as *tooth-ache, air-port* etc. When all the response words could be recalled when given the stimulus words, subjects were presented with a sheet of paper which contained the response words plus an equal number of *new* words which had not appeared in the experiment. The original words had to be indicated. Surprisingly, subjects correctly identified only forty-three out of the forty-eight *old* words despite being able to *recall them all.* That they were unable to recognize five words which they could recall is, of course, contrary to the predictions of the two-process model which cannot accommodate superior recall compared to recognition. Tulving argued that his findings could be explained by resorting to the by now familiar distinction between availability and accessibility. During the learning of the pairs for recall, the stimulus word, e.g. *air*, is present with the response term *port* and the two items are coded together to form what amounts to a *chunk*; the plan for storage and retrieval involves both of them. At recall the stimulus word is presented and acts as an effective retrieval cue for the response thus repeating the finding of Tulving and Osler (see p. 91) that cues are effective if they are present at both storage and retrieval. During recognition, however, the response terms are presented alone so that the conditions are changed from those in effect at storage; as demonstrated by Tulving and Osler, this leads to a failure to gain access to the information available in memory.

We are faced with the paradox that the word *air* is a more effective retrieval cue for the information about *port* than is *port* itself! This is not so surprising when one considers that the word *air* imposes a particular meaning on the word *port* and when the stimulus word of the pair is absent, as in the recognition test, the word may be interpreted differently. For example, *port* may be interpreted as *sea port* or as 'a fortified wine'. Tulving maintains that access to information is not automatic in recognition; even though the stimulus is actually present this does not guarantee that it is interpreted in the same way at presentation and test, and hence the information may be sought out using the wrong retrieval plan.

Summary

Findings that items which cannot be recognized can sometimes be recalled are contrary to the predictions of both the threshold model and the two-process model of recall. While the latter model deals fairly effectively with situations such as those arising from the use of common and uncommon words (p. 100) it does so by assuming that access to available information in memory is direct in recognition tests. Tulving's findings, mentioned directly above, require that both recall and recognition involve retrieval processes, but generally recall is much more dependent on retrieving information which *gives rise* to the word for response, whereas in recognition it is information *about* the word which forms the major part of the task requirements.

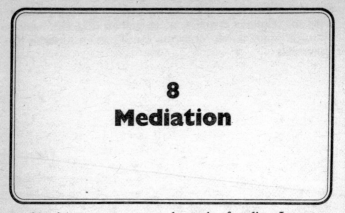

8
Mediation

In this chapter we return to the topic of *coding*. It was explained earlier, in Chapter 6, that information which is to be remembered must be coded into a form which the memory system can 'understand', and the rules used to store these codes must be reapplied if they are to be retrieved. Reduction coding, in which the items to be remembered are reduced to chunks of manageable size and numbers, can be utilized when the items possess sufficient similarities as bases for the construction of such storage and retrieval rules. When the material does not possess such organization, as with the random letter sequence mentioned on page 76, the subjects must find some other way of constructing the necessary rules. The available evidence (some of which is discussed in this chapter) suggests that they do so by incorporating what is essentially nonsense into the existing rules of the memory system. This generally involves some form of *elaboration* of the material.

One of the remarkable things about the human subject is his ability to impose order onto apparently random and meaningless material. This is highlighted by the problems encountered by Ebbinghaus in his classic work mentioned on page 15. This work was directed towards the study of 'pure' learning and forgetting, i.e. uncontaminated by previous learning, and to this end Ebbinghaus learned numerous lists of nonsense syllables and measured the rate at which they were forgotten. He soon realized, however, that although he used items which had no meaning he was unable to prevent them suggesting ideas to him. In effect he had found that nonsense syllables do have a degree of meaningfulness as was pointed out earlier (p. 32) and because of this he was not able to investigate 'pure' learning and forgetting. He was engaged in elaboration coding against his intentions!

The construction and utilization of storage and retrieval rules based on elaboration coding is termed *mediation*. Some examples of mediation will make its meaning clear.

Consider first a task in which the subject is presented with a sequence of three letters, such as L S M, and required to recall them in the correct order (serial recall). This seems a trivial task but as will be seen in Chapter 9 it is indeed difficult to do if the correct steps are taken to prevent rehearsal between seeing the letters and recalling them. Sequences such as L S M which contain three consonants form three chunks in Miller's sense, unlike the trigram G O T which contains three letters but can be reduced to one chunk by forming the word *got*. When the task involves letter sequences which cannot be reduced to a word the subject is faced at recall with the problem of choosing three letters from the alphabet, in the correct order. All the research into verbal memory indicates that the human memory system just does not deal with this type of information in its raw form very well. Instead, the nonsense material has to be incorporated into some existing scheme from semantic memory or some other permanent store of knowledge; it has to be *elaborated* into something meaningful which can be easily retrieved when required. For example, L S M can be elaborated into 'Learn some manners' in which case the trigram has been incorporated into a *verbal mediator* which happens to be an abstract expression – it is difficult to form an image corresponding to it. Alternatively, L S M could be elaborated into 'Lion Sitting on a Mushroom', an example of an *imaginal mediator*. In both cases the stimulus sequence is elaborated by a specific rule into a more easily retrieved form with application of the rule at recall leading to regeneration of the original sequence. Verbal and imaginal mediators are now dealt with in more detail.

Verbal mediation

Two main procedures are used to study verbal mediation. In the first, the experimenter supplies the subjects in the experimental group with the mediator and requires that they use it to learn the material; those in the control group, which have no mediator supplied to them, are required to learn the same material as the experimental group. Differences in performance are attributed to the effects of the mediator. It is often not possible to assume that the control group will not find their own mediators to help them in their task and so they are often given an irrelevant mediator to prevent this occurring. The second class of procedures is concerned with the subject's own derived mediators and involves the requirement that subjects report the mediators they have used. These spontaneous mediators can be verbal or imaginal, the former being known as *Natural Language Mediators*.

Natural Language Mediators

The ways in which Natural Language Mediators (NLMs for short) are formed are indicated by findings from several experiments in which the recall of nonsense trigrams is required. These reveal that more NLMs are reported as being used as the meaningfulness of the material to be recalled increases. It will be remembered that nonsense items do have different levels of meaningfulness as measured by the number of associative responses they elicit (see p. 32) and this suggests that NLMs can be produced via these associations. Associative principles are not the only basis for NLM formation, however, as was shown by Prytulak (quoted by Paivio, 1971) who classified the rules for forming mediators and ordered them according to complexity. Prytulak summarized the basic processes involved in mediation as: (1) the item(s) to be remembered must be transformed into the mediator using a particular rule; (2) the mediator must be stored and recalled; (3) the mediator must be transformed back into the original item. The important point emphasized by Prytulak is that the subject must remember which transformation rule he used for each item in the first stage if he is to regenerate the item in the third stage.

Prytulak's classification of transformation rules included *semantic association* (e.g. LIS to FLEUR as in Fleur de Lis); *semantic phrasing* (MIB to Made In Britain); *substitution*, where a letter is substituted for another (e.g. KAN to CAN); *addition*, where letters are added (e.g. MEL to MEAL); *de-*

letion (e.g. RUK to UK). The rules can be combined: thus, combining *addition* and *deletion* transforms the meaningless MAQ to MAPQ to MAP, while JYZ can be transformed to JAZZ by *substituting* A for Y and *adding* Z. Having recorded the rules used to generate NLMs, Prytulak then went on to investigate how effective these were in regenerating the original items. If the subject is unable to recall the original item it could be due to one or more of three reasons; forgetting the NLM; forgetting the transformation rule; forgetting how to apply the rule even though both it and the NLM are remembered. In order to eliminate the first of these reasons subjects were given the NLMs they said they had formed when endeavouring to learn the items, and were required to transform them back to the items. This procedure therefore tested the subjects' memory, for the transformation rules and how effective these rules are in generating the items. The number of items recalled when given the NLMs was greater when the rules were simple, like addition, than when they were combinations of several rules. One reason for this is that NLMs often directly suggest the type of rule which has been used when the rule is simple. For example, the NLM MEAL suggests *addition* if the items to be remembered were trigrams, and additionally if they were CVC (consonant-vowel-consonant) trigrams then only E or A could have been added. When the rules are combined to give the NLM they are not so readily suggested. It is also possible that subjects try to apply the simple rules to form NLMs and if these fail to produce one they try more complex rules in a certain order. Given the NLM they can then apply the rules, starting with the simplest and continuing until it is possible to generate a sequence which is recognized as the required item. The success in generating the item will decrease with the complexity of the rule combination, not because the rule is not applied, but because the number of possible items generated by complex rules from a given NLM is greater than for simple rules. Essentially there are more sequences to choose from when complex rules are used.

It will doubtless strike the reader that the strategy of producing an NLM is more strewn with hazards than simply remembering the three letters 'by rote'. However, the human memory system just does not deal at all well with nonsense;

it operates much more effectively with units with which it is familiar than with meaningless items.

Manipulation of mediators

Natural Language Mediators are so called because they are produced spontaneously by the subject; hence it is not possible to study the effectiveness of any one mediator by this method because there can be no guarantee that it will be used. The experimenter can obviate this difficulty by instructing the subjects to make use of a particular mediator because they will usually do their best to comply, especially if told that it represents the easiest way to do the task. Dallett (1964) employed this procedure in an experiment involving paired-associate recall. In paired-associate recall the subjects are presented with a number of item pairs (e.g. COR-NIV, WAJ-MEZ) and required to learn them so that when presented with the first item of the pair, the stimulus item (e.g. COR), they can recall the response item (e.g. NIV). Dallett required subjects to learn twelve paired-associates; each containing a nonsense syllable and a word, such as BAC-EGGS. Three groups of subjects were used; the *relevant* group were given a mediator which was relevant to the learning of each pair, e.g. BAC-*bacon*-EGGS (the mediator was presented after the stimulus term and before the response term); the *irrelevant* group were given an irrelevant mediator, e.g. BAC-*bacon*-RETURN; the *control* group were not supplied with a mediator. There was no difference between *relevant* and *control* groups in the recall of the response terms and both were better than the *irrelevant* group. It follows from these findings that the choice of mediator is an important factor in learning paired-associates; also, the finding that *relevant* and *control* groups did not differ in performance can be taken as showing that when left to their own devices subjects are just as capable of deciding what is an effective mediator as is the experimenter.

Further considerations of verbal mediation. In general it is easier to learn items and remember them if they have high, rather than low, meaningfulness. This principle, enunciated by Underwood and Schulz in their extensive study entitled

Meaningfulness and Verbal Learning (1960), implies that as meaningfulness increases it becomes easier to transform the materials into forms more compatible with the established codes of the memory system. There is no guarantee, however, that mediators are only verbal in nature: The coding of BAC-EGGS may be accompanied by a clear visual image of a plate containing bacon and eggs with the result that this image is instrumental in eliciting EGGS in response to BAC. Imaginal mediation is discussed now.

Imaginal mediation

There is considerable evidence that memory performance is improved by instructing the subject to use visual imagery for mediation. When so instructed in a paired-associates task, subjects construct images involving the stimulus and response items, and when presented with the stimulus item can recall the image and extract the response item with remarkable effectiveness. Indeed, if sufficient time is given to form adequate images it is possible for up to 300 paired-associates to be learned in a single presentation sequence. In contrast, ten pairs often prove difficult when verbal coding is employed. Although such remarkable performances are not general, it is clear that imaginal mediation is extremely effective and this is not surprising when the very high levels of retention exhibited by the visual memory system are considered. An impressive demonstration of these levels of retention is provided by Standing, Conezio and Haber (1970). They showed subjects 2560 photographs of scenes for ten seconds each and then presented 280 of them mixed up with 280 *new* photographs. Approximately 90 per cent of the photographs could be correctly recognized as having been shown in the presentation sequence, i.e. something like 2300 pictures, generalizing to the whole list. Incredibly, the accuracy is not much affected when presentation time is reduced to as little as one second! Before using these results as a basis for speculation about the capacity of visual memory to supply effective mediators, it must be realized that they were obtained using the recognition procedure. The ability of the visual memory system to supply effective mediators may be less dramatic when the items must be *recalled*. Despite this, there can be no doubt that imaginal mediation is effective, as we will now show.

The reports given by subjects following memory tests in which they are free to perform whatever coding operations they wish indicate that imagery is commonly occurring. The role played by imagery in memory for words, rather than nonsense items, is indicated by the generally superior performance for words with high imagery values compared to those with low imagery values. It will be remembered that a high imagery value indicates that a clear image can be formed in response to the stimulus word (see p. 51). It is possible, of course, that words differing in imagery value also differ in other ways which affect memorability. High imagery words usually represent concrete objects and hence may be more commonly used in everyday language and this familiarity, rather than imagery, could influence memory performance. Again, imagery value and meaningfulness may vary together without necessarily being causally linked and the latter measure may be responsible for what appears to be an effect of imagery value. Clearly the number of word characteristics which could be confounded with imagery value is large. Allan Paivio has carried out extensive studies to determine whether imagery value or other word characteristics are affecting performance over a range of memory tests and the results are described in his book (Paivio, 1971). He concluded that imagery value has an effect which can be separated from the effects of the other characteristics and was therefore able to distinguish between verbal and imaginal mediation. We will look at one of his studies in detail later in this chapter, but first we must consider some of the ways in which imaginal coding has been used in schemes to improve memory performance. These schemes, known as *mnemonic devices* produce some surprisingly high levels of remembering.

Mnemonic devices

Imaginal coding is so effective in facilitating memory performance that it forms the basis of many mnemonic devices some of which have been in use since the times of the early Greek civilisation. Essentially they are based on the provision of a well-established plan in the form of visual images, into which images corresponding to the to-be-remembered objects are placed. Two of the most commonly used devices are discussed to illustrate the principles involved.

Method of Loci. This device is attributed to Simonides who lived in Greece about 500 B.C. Cicero, in *De Oratore*, tells that Simonides was invited to a banquet to recite a poem as part of the entertainment. Following his recitation he was called outside to speak to a messenger and meanwhile the building collapsed killing everyone inside. Relatives of the dead found it impossible to recognize the remains under the rubble but Simonides was able to identify them by reinstating the image of the hall, 'searching through it', and identifying the bodies according to the positions of people in the image. Simonides was so impressed with his ability to remember in this way that he devised the Method of Loci to assist remembering in more usual circumstances. In this device, objects which are to be remembered are imaged as vividly as possible and placed in specific places in a room. If a shopping list is to be remembered, for example, the image of loaf may be placed by the door, a packet of sugar by the window, and so on. At the time of recall in the shop, the places are inspected for the images they contain. It is not necessary to use a room in which to place the objects; the parts of a building or a row of shops of various descriptions could be used. The important point is that the same set of positions must be used on every occasion and in the same order because the loci act as 'cues'; the items to be remembered are paired with the cues through elaborative coding in which the item is converted to an image and this then combined with the cue image. At recall, the cue is readily remembered, being part of the long-established scheme, and the item is retrieved with the cue.

Pegword method. Principles similar to those just outlined apply to the pegword method in which the *loci* are replaced by the images of unrelated objects. As a means of maintaining the objects in a constant order they are chosen so that their names rhyme with the first twenty or so integers. For example, *bun* may be chosen to represent the first peg because it rhymes with *one*; *shoe* goes with *two*; *three-tree*; *four-door* etc. The objects represented by the *pegwords* provide the images which form the basis for elaborating the to-be-

111

remembered objects by combining the images. Given the sequence *flag, horse, car, book,* the corresponding images may be combined with the pegword images so the first combination produces a large current bun with a flag flying from a pole stuck in the top of it; the second combination could be a horse wearing shoes; and so on. The pegword method has an advantage not enjoyed by the Method of Loci in that it enables the user to recall the item presented in a given serial position without the necessity to count round the *loci* in order. All the pegword user must do is transform the number of the serial position into its pegword and this into its image which will be retrieved in combination with the image of the required item. The pegword method, like the Method of Loci, combines the long-lasting properties of the imaginal code with well-established retrieval cues, in this case the first twenty or so integers. Thus the rules according to which the information is stored are easily reapplied and the information retrieved.

The pegword method has been extensively studied by Gordon Bower of Stanford University (see Bower, 1970) who found that more than one item can be hung on each peg. For example, the items *flag, horse, car* and *book* may be combined into an image of a horse, reading a book and sitting in a car, the body of which is made of a large bun with a flag flying from the front. While it is possible to remember twenty items with twenty pegs, or with five pegs and four items per peg, the latter method will almost certainly lead to a loss of information about the order in which the items are presented. In addition, the ability to use one peg for several items only holds if the items are presented together and simultaneously integrated with the peg. Bower demonstrated this by requiring three groups of subjects to learn the same twenty words but with instructions to use twenty, ten or four pegwords. The pegwords were presented with only one item at a time so, for instance, each pegword in the four-peg condition was presented five times, each time with a different item; subjects were instructed to use imagery to associate the pegword and the items. Performance fell dramatically as the number of words per peg increased. It is not certain why this occurs, but possibly the subjects form a different image for a particular peg-word on each of its several occurrences. Thus, each to-be-remembered item is stored with a different cue. At recall, a subject attempting to recall all the items combined with the image of a bun, and using only one image of a bun as a retrieval cue, will fail to retrieve items whose images are stored with other images of a bun.

The reasons why information coded in terms of imagery is so effectively stored and retrieved are not clear, but most people, with practice, can achieve surprising levels of performance using mnemonic schemes. More extensive discussion of such schemes is provided by Paivio (1971).

Separating verbal and imaginal mediation
Mnemonic schemes such as the Method of Loci and the peg-word method work well provided the items to be remembered can be converted into images. This can be done when the intention is to remember all the items on a shopping list but not very adequate when abstract words are involved and there is difficulty generating corresponding images. Furthermore, images take time to generate and so, when the items to be remembered are presented rapidly, the subjects may have time only to generate verbal codes.

The existence of imaginal and verbal codes leads to several interesting questions. Concrete words, which refer to concrete objects, e.g. *table*, are usually more easily remembered than abstract words which represent abstract concepts, e.g. *justice*. Does this difference arise because imaginal coding is superior to verbal coding, or because concrete words have the benefit of both codes while abstract words have the benefit of only one? The latter position is known as the *dual-trace hypothesis* because two forms of coding are utilized together for concrete words.

Allan Paivio and his colleague K. Csapo have conducted experiments which support the dual-trace hypothesis by showing that concrete words give superior performance to abstracts when there is sufficient opportunity to form images, otherwise this superiority is small or even reversed. The logic behind Paivio's research is as follows. Verbal stimuli (words) can be coded verbally more rapidly than images can be formed for imaginal coding; pictures of objects, however, should be more rapidly coded in imaginal terms because the basis of such coding is directly available in the stimulus itself; the verbal code must await the retrieval of the appropriate name for the picture. Consider first situations in which the rate of presentation of to-be-remembered *words* is varied; the picture stimuli will be discussed later. At fast presentation rates, there will be insufficient time to form images to concrete words and so any advantage derived from imaginal coding will be eliminated; both concrete and abstract words will rely on verbal coding and they should differ little on memorability. When slow rates of presentation are used there will be adequate time for image-formation and concrete words should have an advantage. Paivio and Csapo showed this to be so.

The effect of reducing the rate at which the *pictorial* stimuli were presented was to improve performance on memory tests much more than the corresponding increase with words. This is consistent with the view that the longer time available enabled the slower process of verbal coding to be completed in addition to imaginal coding. Importantly, the increase in performance was more dramatic in free recall and recognition than in tests of serial recall. The difference between these tasks is their dependence on memory for the *order* in which the items are presented; serial recall requires that the items be recalled in the correct order while free recall and recognition test whether the subject can remember if the item was in the list or not, irrespective of order. The dramatic increases in free recall and recognition with longer presentation time obtained for pictures indicates that imaginal codes are more effective than verbal codes in remembering whether an item occurred in the presentation list or not. That verbal codes are more effective in dealing with *order* information is suggested by the findings that abstract words give better performance than concrete words on serial recall, provided that subjects are not engaged in the use of devices such as the pegword mnemonic!

Summary

Mediation is best seen as a means of incorporating material which lacks organization of its own into storage and retrieval plans provided by semantic memory and other long-term stores of information. Use of mediators is necessary because the memory system finds it difficult to deal with material which does not conform to its existing coding rules. The distinction between verbal and imaginal forms of coding is supported by subjective reports and experimental evidence such as that provided by Paivio. Employment of imaginal coding in mnemonic devices can lead to remarkable levels of remembering, suggesting that the capacity of visual imaginal memory to record episodic phenomena is very great.

9
Forgetting

Forgetting is one of the most frustrating aspects of life. We spend much of our time trying to learn facts and skills and often find that we are unable to remember them at the crucial moment. Forgetting has its advantages as well as its disadvantages, however; one of the important features of the peripheral stores and primary memory is the rapid loss of information held in them so that other information can be stored. Similarly, in the longer term, it is necessary to forget facts which have become out-dated and have to be replaced with new ones.

The evidence about *forgetting* and the explanation of it should have something to contribute to our understanding of *remembering*: any comprehensive theory of memory must account for both. One theory of remembering which has been emphasized in several earlier chapters maintains that if remembering is to occur the rules used to store the information must also be employed at retrieval. Failure to remember will be evidenced to the extent that the rules employed at the two stages differ from each other. This theory attributes forgetting to failures in the retrieval process. Other theories of forgetting emphasize changes taking place in the memory store during the retention interval.

Before laying the blame for failures to remember on *forgetting* it is necessary to rule out the possibility that the material *was not learned* in the first place. Clearly, what has not been learned cannot be forgotten! Because of this, *for-*

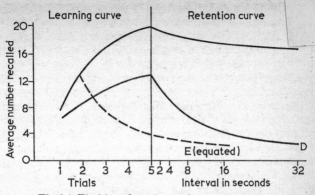

Fig 9.1 *Fictitious learning and retention curves*

getting is defined as taking place when something which can be remembered at one time cannot be remembered at a later time.

Learning and forgetting

Figure 9.1 contains fictitious curves to illustrate the effects of level of learning on retention and are typical of experiments in which subjects are required to learn a list of twenty words for recall. One list, E, is an easy list to learn (e.g. containing highly associated words) and list D is a difficult list (unrelated words). One group of subjects learn list E, another group learn list D. They are given five trials each consisting of a presentation of the list followed by free recall, and the numbers of words recalled are represented by the *learning curve* on the left of Figure 9.1. On the fifth trial group E can recall more words than group D, as would be expected. Subjects are then given another recall test (but no further presentation of the lists) after two, four, eight, sixteen *or* thirty-two minutes. The numbers of words recalled at each interval are shown on the right of Figure 9.1, the *retention curve*.

It can be seen that curve D falls more rapidly than curve E; that is, the *rate of forgetting* is greater for the lower curve. Is it possible to conclude from this that lists of unrelated words are forgotten more rapidly than lists of associated words? The answer is *No*! The E list was learned more thoroughly than the D list and differences in the rates of forgetting are possibly due to this, rather than the type of list. Level of learning and type of list are *confounded*, and it is not possible to separate the effects of one from those of the other. In order to compare the rates of forgetting for the two types of lists it is necessary to equate the levels of learning at the start of the retention interval. This can be done by continuing the learning trials on list D until performance is perfect, or by terminating the trials on list E so that it is equivalent to that of list D at the start of the retention interval, e.g. at Trial 2 for E and Trial 5 for D. The forgetting curve for list E, when learning is terminated after Trial 2, is shown as E (equated) in Figure 9.1 and has been given the same shape as curve D. The conclusions which follow from this particular situation are (1) when the two lists are equated for level of learning, the rates of forgetting are the same, and (2) the higher the level of learning at the start of the retention interval, the lower the rate of forgetting, i.e. comparing curve E with E (equated).

Causes of forgetting

Attempts to explain forgetting fall largely into three main theories; trace decay, interference, and retrieval failure. Trace decay is based on the concept of the memory trace, i.e. when an item is perceived and learned, a trace is formed in the brain tissues involved in memory storage. The trace may take the form of neural activity which gradually dies away unless reactivated by further presentations of the item, or by rehearsal. The threshold model of recall and recognition (see p. 96) is based on the notion that if the trace becomes too weak it will not contain sufficient information for the item to be remembered.

Interference theory maintains that memory is based on the formation of associations and learning one set of associations involving an item interferes with learning other associations involving it. To take a simple example, recently-married women often find difficulty in giving their married name rather than their maiden name; the long established habit of giving the maiden name interferes with the newly-learned association.

The retrieval failure explanation of forgetting has already

been discussed in Chapter 6 when a distinction was made between storage and retrieval; information which is not accessible at one time may be accessible when adequate retrieval cues are provided. According to this explanation, when an item can be recalled on the *first* occasion but not on the second, forgetting occurs because the correct retrieval plan is not used on the second occasion. This theory has the advantage of explaining situations in which performance actually *improves* with increasing retention interval; it does so simply by maintaining that the items became accessible on the second attempt through use of the *correct* retrieval cues, incorrect ones having been used on the first attempt.

Each theory has had its strong advocates who have insisted that it is the only explanation of forgetting but, as is usual in psychological research, one explanation may seem appropriate in one situation while another explanation best accounts for other situations. For a long time it was believed that forgetting in short-term memory (over a period of seconds) is accounted for by decay, while with longer intervals it is due to interference. Recently, due mainly to an influential paper by Melton (1963), it has been recognized that the distinction between short-term and long-term memory cannot be maintained on this basis because interference explanations do seem appropriate in many short-term tasks. Each of the three theories is now discussed in more detail.

Decay

The decay theory of forgetting has an intuitive appeal about it. It seems to describe the way in which certain types of memories fade away, as for example the memory of an auditory tone, or the sensation of being touched. Decay in the activity of nervous tissue may directly account for such experiences but decay theory is difficult to test for verbal materials because of the need to equate all aspects of the experimental situation except the opportunity for decay. The basic experimental test of the theory simply involves testing different groups of subjects after different retention intervals. This plan has problems associated with it, however, because if the subjects are merely left to their own devices they will almost certainly rehearse the material and will show little forgetting, if any! If attempts are made to prevent rehearsal by forcing the subjects to engage in some activity during the retention interval, the amount of activity increases directly with the interval, and any loss of performance could be due to interference from this activity rather than decay of the memory trace.

Decay in long-term memory. Jenkins and Dallenbach (1924) pointed out that decay theory predicts a constant rate of forgetting irrespective of the activity undertaken in the interval. They tested this prediction by having subjects learn lists of nonsense syllables and requiring recall after various intervals of either sleep or normal working activity. Forgetting was most rapid for the normal-activity group and this was taken to indicate that interference from everyday activity was largely responsible for forgetting, and not decay, which should produce equal forgetting rates. Several problems arise with this type of procedure, the most important being the difficulty in ensuring that sleep is attained rapidly after the list is learned. If subjects are awake they may engage in activity which makes the items resistant to decay; the activity group may have no such opportunity.

Rather more control can be achieved by using sensory deprivation instead of sleep. Here the experimental subjects are confined in a sound-proof room and all forms of stimulation are minimized. Another group of subjects are free to go about their normal activities. In tests of the decay theory of forgetting, both groups learn a list of items to the same level of recall and are tested again after intervals under the appropriate conditions. Results usually show that the confined group forgets least even though they do not expect the final test and hence are not likely to rehearse during their inactivity. These findings support the conclusions of Jenkins and Dallenbach that decay is not a major source of forgetting over long intervals of time.

Decay in short-term memory. Conrad has several times suggested that telephone numbers are difficult to dial because the dialling procedure is slow and permits decay to take place. He conducted an experiment to test this (Conrad, 1957) and included conditions in which subjects were required to recall sequences of eight digits in the correct order (serial recall). In one condition the digits were presented at a rate of $\frac{2}{3}$ seconds per digit with recall being paced at the same speed. In a second, slow condition, presentation and recall were at 2 seconds per digit. Because recall was serial the interval between presentation and recall of each digit was about 5.3 seconds in the fast condition and 16 seconds in the slow condition but, of course, the conditions did not differ in the *contents* of those intervals: the same number of presentations and recalls occurred in each. Performance was best in the fast condition as predicted by the decay theory.

Nancy Waugh and Donald Norman produced evidence differing somewhat from Conrad's. In their study (from which they derived their concept of primary memory, see Ch. 5) they presented lists of sixteen digits at a rate of either one per second or four per second. The last digit, known as the *probe digit* had occurred exactly once before in the list and the task was to recall the digit which had followed it. Basically, Waugh and Norman found that the ability to recall the required item decreased as the number of items intervening between its presentation and recall increased, but this fall in performance was nearly the same for both presentation rates. They could argue, therefore, that forgetting was caused by the intervening items rather than decay, but forgetting was not quite so great for the fast as for the slow rate, this suggesting that decay may have contributed to the effect.

The Brown–Peterson Technique. John Brown, working at Cambridge in the 1950s, and L. R. and M. J. Peterson working in America, introduced a technique consisting of three stages: (1) presentation of a small number of items to be remembered, usually three items presented together for two or three seconds; (2) a retention interval of up to eight seconds filled with a *distractor task* to prevent rehearsal of the items (often counting backwards in threes from a given number); (3) recall of the items in the original order. The data collected with this procedure are fairly orderly and are represented in Figure 9.2. Decay is a possible explanation of the forgetting observed, but so is interference since the amount of intervening activity increases directly with the length of the retention interval. Interference of this sort, arising from materials encountered between learning the to-be-remembered set of items and recalling them, is known as *retroactive interference*

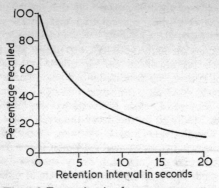

Fig. 9.2 *Forgetting in short-term memory*

because it has the *appearance* of acting backwards; the distractor task appears to interfere with the memory for a set of items presented earlier. This explanation does not seem relevant here because there is no reason why the counting backwards task should produce such massive interference in a task containing a different class of items, i.e. words rather than digits. Decay then seems the best explanation of forgetting in this situation and that was the view widely held until Keppel and Underwood in America showed that interference could not be ruled out. Their experiment is now used to introduce a section on interference as a source of forgetting.

Interference

Proactive interference. Evidence that decay is not an adequate explanation of forgetting in the Brown–Peterson technique came from two experiments conducted by Keppel and Underwood (1962). In one of these they used the Brown–Peterson procedure of testing serial recall of consonant trigrams (e.g. CXP) after 3, 9 and 18 seconds of backwards counting. Some subjects had the intervals tested in the order 3, 9, 18, others had 9, 3, 18, and so on, so that the order of testing was balanced up. The important feature of the results appears when only the first trial for each subject is considered (some had intervals of 3 seconds, others 9, others 18 on this trial). No forgetting takes places, performance is near 100 per cent for all intervals. When the second and third trials are taken separately, performance falls steadily as the interval increases. If decay is the sole explanation of forgetting performance should fall as the interval increases on the first trial as it does on later trials. Keppel and Underwood suggested that learning the first trigram interfers with learning the second one, and learning the first two interferes with the third. The first item learned in the experiment is not forgotten because there are no preceding items to interfere with it. This type of interference is known as *proactive interference* because it appears to act forwards, earlier learning interfering with later learning. Keppel and Underwood showed that proactive interference builds up as more and more lists are learned and some interesting features of this build-up have been revealed by the studies of D. Wickens whose findings are now briefly discussed.

Release from proactive interference. The build-up of proactive interference in the Brown–Peterson situation is particularly rapid if the three items to be remembered on each trial are taken from the same class, e.g. they are always digits, or always the names of birds. If on the fourth trial (for example) the class of item is changed to letters instead of digits, or to trees instead of birds, performance improves dramatically. This situation is depicted in Figure 9.3. Line C is typical of

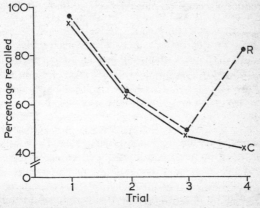

Fig. 9.3 *Release from proactive interference*

123

performance for a *control* group who have the class of items unchanged on the fourth trial; performance continues to decline. Line R shows the *release from proactive interference* which occurs when the class *is* changed.

Wickens (1972) has reviewed a number of studies of the release phenomenon and concluded that many types of change will produce the effect. In addition to the examples given above, changes in the imagery value of words, the modality of presentation (auditory-visual), ratings on the semantic differential (see p. 26) and even changes in the background on which the words are presented, will all produce release.

A rather obvious explanation of the release effect is that subjects are alerted by the change in the class of materials to be remembered. Certainly, release does occur if the subject is told on the final trial that a change *may* take place, even though the class is *not* changed. The warning makes the subject pay careful attention to the items. This does not provide a complete explanation of release because it occurs when no warning is given and when subjects are not aware that any change has taken place. Wickens believes that the findings can be explained if it is assumed that the rules the subjects use to store items and retrieve them involve certain of the items' features as explained in Chapter 6. When the items on all trials belong to the same class these rules, being used repeatedly, lose their effectiveness for retrieving the items on the current trial; they become over-worked, in effect, and performance falls accordingly. When the class is changed on the final trial new rules, not overworked, can be employed and the release effect occurs. Wickens makes the important point that any type of change in the materials which produces release must also be involved in the rules used to store and retrieve them. Hence the release from proactive interference can be used to look at the coding rules employed.

Measuring interference. Decay theory is unable to account for the increased forgetting which occurs in the Brown–Peterson technique as the number of previous lists learned increases. It is also unable to account for Jenkins and Dallenbach's results. Instead, the results are attributed to either learning earlier lists, to activity intervening between learning and recall, or to a combination of both. The earlier learning is said to *interfere* with later learning (proactive interference), and the intervening activity to *interfere* with remembering the items learned prior to it (retroactive interference). *Retroactive* is not a good name for the latter type of interference because it is not possible for anything to work backwards in time; the effects must be due to interference with information already stored by the time the intervening activity starts, or with the process of retrieval *after* the intervening activity has been completed.

A vast number of experiments have been conducted to investigate the circumstances under which interference occurs and what determines its magnitude. The variety of experimental manipulations which have been investigated is too great to allow any extensive coverage here. Instead, a general coverage of one basic approach is given and this will be discussed in relation to interference theory, until recently a widely accepted explanation of forgetting.

The basic experimental plans for the assessment of interference are shown in Table 9.1.

Table 9.1

Plans for the assessment of interference.

	Group	Stage 1	Interval 1	Stage 2	Interval 2	Stage 3
Proactive interference	Experimental	Learn A	—	Learn B	—	Test B
	Control	X	—	Learn B	—	Test B
Retroactive interference	Experimental	Learn A	—	Learn B	—	Test A
	Control	Learn A	—	X	—	Test A

For the sake of brevity proactive and retroactive interference will be referred to as PI and RI respectively.

In Table 9.1, A and B represent lists of to-be-remembered items. In the PI conditions the experimental group learns list A, then learns list B and finally is tested on B. If PI is present the final performance on B will be less than if A had not been learned. The control group provides an estimate of how well the experimental group would have done had there been no interference from A. This is so, because X in stage 1 consists either of learning nothing (subjects are just left to their own pursuits) or they are required to learn materials which will not interfere with A, e.g. if A consists of words then X may be learning lists of digits. The inclusion of a learning task has the advantage of ensuring that the control group has as much chance to 'warm up' as the experimental group had by learning A. Differences between the two groups at stage 3 give a measure of PI.

In the RI conditions, it is the task learned at stage 1 which is tested at stage 3. If X is again a learning task containing materials unrelated to A, then it equates the two groups for opportunity to rehearse or otherwise 'think about' A. Differences in scores at stage 3 indicate the effect of learning B on retention of A.

Several aspects of the basic plans can be varied and the effects on interference observed. These variables include the length of both intervals, 1 and 2; the type of materials in A and B (letters, words, digits) and the similarity of items in the two sets; and the extent to which A and B are learned. The tests used to measure learning in stages 1 and 2, and the amount retained at stage 3, can be any of the accepted memory procedures and each will reveal something unique about interference. There is only space here to discuss one test and recall of paired-associates is chosen because it is relatively easy to show how results obtained with it relate to interference theory. This is briefly described below.

The task chosen for illustration involves learning number-word paired-associates with A (in Table 9.1) containing pairs such as *24 – House*; *19 – Road* etc. In this particular task B contains the same *stimulus* terms as A but different *response* terms, e.g. *24 – Cat*; *19 – Honey*. As may be expected on an intuitive basis, PI increases as A is more adequately learned, i.e. recall of B deteriorates as A is given more learning trials. Similarly, RI increases as interference learning of B is carried further. There were two major explanations of these effects in existence around the year 1940, and these are briefly mentioned now.

Explanations of Interference. J. A. McGeoch proposed that when subjects have been required to learn two responses to the same stimulus there is competition between them at stage 3. The amount of competition put up by each response depends on the extent to which it has been learned; so, for example, if B is well learned at stage 2 there will be little PI because A responses, learned less well, will be unable to com-

126

pete successfully; the amount of RI will *increase* because B will be able to compete successfully with the A responses which are required at stage 3.

In contrast to McGeoch's view, Melton and Irwin proposed that learning the B responses to the stimulus terms led to *unlearning* of the A responses so they actually became unavailable.

Barnes and Underwood (1959) pointed out that if the learning of one set of responses led to unlearning of the others then, if the subjects are required to recall *both* of them at stage 3, recall of A responses should decrease as recall of B responses increases. They varied the number of trials given to learn B (at stage 2) and found that recall of A did decrease as B increased, thus supporting the unlearning theory. Since then there has been evidence to show that these results do not always hold and other problems for both theories have been found. Because of this there is at present no strongly held version of interference theory (see Postman and Underwood, 1973, for a full account of the problems). Apart from the problems encountered by interference theory in explaining the results of experiments using the plans outlined in Table 9.1 it also suffers as a general theory of forgetting because the situations it best deals with are rarely encountered in everyday life; how often do we have to learn similar verbal responses to the same stimuli within a short period of time?

Cue-dependent forgetting
Much of Chapters 6, 7 and 8 have been devoted to showing that information which is available in memory will not be accessible if the correct retrieval rules are not followed. For example, Tulving and Pearlstone showed that provision of the category name, supplied with the word at presentation, was effective in bringing about recall of items which could not be recalled without it. It is not necessary to repeat the arguments made in those chapters but one or two additional points remain to be made.

Decay theory has difficulty dealing with situations where items which cannot be remembered at one time can be remembered at a future time even though no additional presentations have been made. It can be argued that providing the cue, which is semantically related in some way to the item, leads to an addition to the trace strength of the item (and other related items) and this leads to the enhanced performance. This view can be rejected as a general explanation because of results obtained with what is known as the multi-trial free recall procedure. In this procedure subjects are given a single presentation of a list and asked for free recall. Then with no further presentations, and with the responses from the first attempt removed, they are given a second and then a third attempt. It is found (Tulving, 1968) that some items not recalled on Trial 1 are recalled on Trial 2, and some items not recalled on Trial 1 or Trial 2 are recalled on Trial 3. No additional cues have been given to 'push up' the trace strength and yet items inaccessible at one time become accessible later on. These effects can be explained if it is assumed that the subjects use slightly different retrieval plans on successive trials. This would also explain the additional finding that some items which are recalled on Trials 1 and 2 are *not* recalled on Trial 3. The change in retrieval cues has led to forgetting, but forgetting arising from loss of access rather than availability. This last-mentioned finding is difficult for both decay and interference theories to explain.

In a clear exposition of the cue-dependent theory of forgetting Tulving (1974) points out several inadmissible criticisms often levelled against it. One of these is that the theory maintains that all information entered into the memory system remains available, i.e. forgetting is entirely due to retrieval failure. The theory need make no such claim: it is possible to maintain that a large amount of forgetting is best explained by retrieval failure without having to maintain that no other sources of forgetting exist. Another criticism has been that cue-dependent forgetting explains the effectiveness of cues in bringing about retrieval of otherwise 'forgotten' items, but it does not explain why the cues are 'forgotten'. Are they also dependent on other cues for their retrieval and so on *ad infinitum*? Tulving points out that it is not necessary that the cues themselves be remembered; they can be provided by outside sources such as the general experimental environment or Penfield's electrical stimulation of the brain tissue.

Failures to remember are experienced by everybody and are part of normal everyday life. Sometimes these failures occur because the facts or events were not considered very important and were not learned, i.e. not stored in memory. Other failures to remember may be due to tiredness at the time of remembering, or to distraction by other events going on at the time. Occasionally such failures are due to embarrassment or disappointment associated with the events and the individual chooses not to remember them because of the unpleasantness attached to them. More serious failures of memory arise from damage to the brain or from particularly severe emotional shock associated with a specific event. In the latter case the individual may be completely unable to recall the event which nevertheless continues to influence his behaviour, sometimes in such a disruptive manner that he must seek therapeutic help. This phenomenon of *repression* is featured in Frieud's theory of personality. Because the effect is not easily dealt with by the experimental techniques stressed in this book it will not be discussed here; but it is discussed in Volume D3 of this series, and George Talland (1968) deals with it in a very readable account. Talland also deals with amnesia, the loss of memory which occurs as a result of certain types of damage to the brain. Williams (1970) also gives an introduction to this topic which can be investigated experimentally and which is briefly described now.

Amnesia

Memory disorders can arise from damage to the brain as a result of accident or disease, or from the normal effects of ageing. This damage can come about rapidly as a result of blows to the head, such as occur in road accidents, or by the progressive effects of alcoholism or the growth of tumours. The sort of disorders which the damage produces depends on the amount of brain tissue damaged and the part of the brain affected. Memory disorders are most prevalent where the *temporal lobes* at the sides of the brain are damaged. Amnesia is the name given to conditions in which the patient has a loss of some of his ability to remember, but is clearly conscious, aware of what is going on around him, able to hold conversations, and performs normally on most intelligence tests. Thus, amnesia is separated from conditions in which language, thinking, recognition of objects and other cognitive abilities in addition to memory are affected.

The experimental study of memory disorders is carried out to determine which aspect of memory is affected, storage or retrieval, and which part of the brain is involved. In addition to indicating ways in which the patient's symptoms may be relieved, such investigations provide insight into the working of the brain and the nature of memory processes.

Amnesia occurs in two forms which usually appear together: *retrograde* amnesia is present when events occurring before the *trauma* (event in which the damage takes place) cannot be remembered; *anterograde* amnesia is present when events following the trauma cannot be remembered.

Retrograde amnesia. Accidental blows to the head often cause loss of consciousness. Recovery of consciousness is usually followed by a period in which memory does not function, and when it does begin to function there is a loss of the ability to recall events taking place before the trauma. The ability gradually returns with events from the remote past being remembered first, and the period covered by the amnesia progressively shrinks until quite recent events can be remembered. Sometimes the period of amnesia extends over years: Professor Zangwill of Cambridge has reported a patient who, when asked to draw a present-day public transport vehicle with a woman in it, drew the vehicle and the woman's clothes as they would have been fifteen years before the onset of amnesia; she could not recall the styles from the intervening years. If the trauma is not too severe it is usually possible for the patient eventually to recall events up to a few seconds before it.

The recovery of the ability to recall events indicates that the stored information is not destroyed but that there has been a temporary loss of the ability to retrieve it. The information is available all the time but access to it has been disrupted. This view is supported by the findings that occasionally the patient can recall an isolated event from the amnesic period and can do this shortly after the trauma but not when recovery is more complete; here the information is shown to be available and accessible at one time but not accessible later on.

Anterograde amnesia. This describes the condition in which the patient has difficulty learning new skills or facts, or remembering day-to-day events occurring after the trauma. For example, Brenda Milner of Canada reported a patient who was able to mow the lawn regularly but could not remember where the mower was kept. He could perform the long-established skill of mowing but could not learn the new fact, where the mower was kept. Amnesic patients are able to perform short-term memory tasks involving small numbers of items as well as can normal subjects. It is tempting to conclude from this that they suffer an inability to transfer information from primary memory to secondary memory (see Ch. 5). However, they are often able to improve their performance when they are given help in the form of retrieval cues, this suggesting that some of the anterograde amnesia is due to failure of the retrieval process rather than the storage process.

Summary

Three theories of forgetting have been discussed. Decay theory receives little support outside the area of short-term memory extending over a few seconds and involving digits as the to-be-remembered items; even in this small area its validity is disputed. The concepts of response-competition and unlearning have not been clearly stated by supporters of interference theory, nor have they received consistent experimental support. The most embracing theory of forgetting is that based on cue-dependency. The notion that information is not retrieved because the appropriate cues are not used fits in with the broad distinction between availability and accessibility pursued in Chapters 6 and 7. The recovery of memory for events preceding traumatic blows to the head demonstrates that the forgetting in retrograde amnesia is due to failure to gain access to the available information. Defects in both storage and retrieval processes account for anterograde amnesia.

131

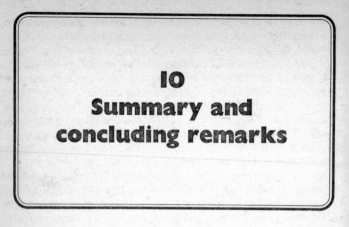

10
Summary and concluding remarks

Summary

Memory is involved when experiences at one time are carried forward to affect behaviour at a later time. It is important to distinguish between the several connotations given to the word *memory*. These are: (1) the memory *system*, i.e. the 'mechanisms' which perform the memory processes; (2) the *contents* of the memory stores, i.e. the representations of past experiences stored in the memory system; (3) memory *performance*, i.e. the ability to remember.

The contents of this book are concerned with the *experimental* study of human memory. Although it has not been possible to do more than sample the enormous amount of research carried out on the topic, the intention has been to introduce the procedures generally used, the nature of the observations made, and the way in which conclusions about the working of the memory system are derived from them.

The principles of good experimentation include *control* of any aspect of the experimental situation which may vary so that *observed* changes in behaviour can be attributed to the manipulations made by the experimenter. It should have become apparent to the reader by now that *memory*, in the sense of the *system*, cannot be observed directly. What can be observed are the experimental conditions and the subjects' responses; the characteristics of the component parts of the system have to be inferred from changes in the latter brought about by changes in the former. This method of inference has been emphasized throughout the book but particularly detailed attention was given to it in Chapters 3 and 5; Chapter 3 contained a detailed discussion of attempts to explain the results of semantic decision-making tasks by models based on the structural features of the memory stores, or which make assumptions about the decision process, while the inferential steps involved in the derivation of the characteristics of primary memory are detailed in Chapter 5.

Everyday experience indicates that the human memory system is remarkably versatile. It is able to store and give access to the information necessary for overt and covert activities including: comprehension and production of spoken and written language symbols; the recognition of objects; thinking; imagery, i.e. the recall of sensory experiences in both the waking and sleeping states; motor skills, such as walking; and the remembering of events or episodes.

The selection and organization of evidence in the preceding chapters reflects a particular and widely-held view about the memory system, but not the only one (see Craik and Lockhart, 1972). The view held here maintains that the memory system consists of a series of stores (peripheral, primary, and secondary) which enable information reaching the sensory receptors to be transformed into progressively more durable codes. In order to record episodes involving verbal materials the subject must call upon semantic memory, or imaginal memory, to provide the basis for the construction of retrieval plans by the use of either elaboration or reduction coding. Although the amount of information which can be stored in secondary memory is large there are limits on the rates at which coding for storage can take place and at which retrieval can proceed. If it takes *cognitive work* to carry out these processes then the *capacity* of the subject to perform this work is limited. This agrees with the widely accepted view of man as a *limited capacity processing* system (see A1, A4, A5 and Broadbent 1971).

The human subject is not a passive recipient of sensory impressions; he is not a wax tablet, nor a tape recorder; nor even a computer! Remembering is not merely a replaying of some direct record of experience; rather the subject has to reconstruct the episodes from indirect representations or codes, as Professor (later Sir) Frederic Bartlett pointed out (see Bartlett, 1932). While it is convenient to use analogies for the purpose of bringing order to the observations made in research, it must not be forgotten that the evidence is obtained from *individuals*. They differ in their ability to remember in a variety of ways and for a variety of reasons, even in a carefully selected group of experimental subjects. Individuals not selected in any special way differ in ability to remember to a remarkable extent; from the total amnesic to the mnemonist, discussed by Luria in his book *The Mind of a Mnemonist*, who was able to perform quite abnormally well on memory tasks. The reasons for these individual differences include genetic factors, disease, accident, educational background and emotional factors. These represent important areas of investigation for the psychologist, educationist and therapist but they have been given scant consideration here because of lack of space. Instead, emphasis has been placed on the scientific procedures and principles which must provide a basis for the investigation of the role these factors play in memory ability.

Further reading

These suggestions for further reading are arranged alphabetically and the chapters to which they are relevant are shown in brackets. Where the book gives a wide coverage of the field of memory it is indicated by *G*, and any specific chapters which are covered in detail in such books are also given.

Brown, J. (to appear summer 1975) *Recognition and Recall.* New York: Wiley. (7)

Cermak, L. S. (1972) *Human Memory: Research and Theory.* New York: Ronald (*G*, 1)

Herriot, P. (1974) *Attributes of Memory.* London: Methuen. (*G*, 2, 3, 6)

Jung, J. (1968) *Verbal Learning.* New York: Holt, Rinehart and Winston. (*G*, 8, 9)

Kausler, D. H. (1974) *Psychology of Verbal Learning and Memory.* New York: Academic Press. (*G*)

Kintsch, W. (1970) *Learning, Memory, and Conceptual Processes.* New York: Academic Press. (6, 9)

Lyons, J. (ed.) (1970) *New Horizons in Linguistics.* Harmondsworth: Penguin. (2)

Melton, A. W. and Martin, E. (eds.) (1972) *Coding Processes in Human Memory.* New York: Winston. (6, 9)

Murdock, B. B. (1974) *Human Memory: Theory and Data.* Potomac: Laurence Erlbaum. (5, 7)

Norman, D. A. (ed.) (1970) *Models of Human Memory.* New York: Academic Press. (1, 5, 7)

Paivio, A. (1971) *Imagery and Verbal Processes.* New York: Holt, Rinehart and Winston. (*G*, 4, 8)

Richardson, A. (1969) *Mental Imagery*. London: Routledge and Kegan Paul. (4)

Sheehan, P. W. (ed.) (1972) *The Function and Nature of Imagery*. New York: Academic Press. (4)

Summerfield, A. (ed.) (1971) *Cognitive Psychology, British Medical Bulletin 27*, no. 3. Papers by Craik (5), Baddeley and Patterson (5), Warrington (9), Morton (2)

Talland, G. A. (1965) *Deranged Memory*. New York: Academic Press. (9)

Talland, G. A. (ed.) (1968) *Human Ageing and Behaviour*. New York: Academic Press. (9)

Tulving, E. and Donaldson, W. A. (eds.) (1972) *Organisation of Memory*. New York: Academic Press. (*G*, 2, 3, 6)

Books of readings

The books listed below contain reprints of original papers. Where a paper referred to in the present book is contained in one of these books of readings it is indicated in the References section.

Coltheart, M. (ed.) (1972) *Readings in Cognitive Psychology*. Toronto: Holt, Rinehart and Winston.

Gardiner, J. M. (ed.) (forthcoming) *Readings in Human Memory*. London: Methuen.

Postman, L. and Keppel, G. (eds.) (1969) *Verbal Learning and Memory*. Harmondsworth: Penguin.

Slamecka, N. J. (1967) *Human Learning and Memory: Selected Readings*. New York: Oxford University Press.

References
and Name Index

The numbers in italics following each entry refer to page numbers within this book.

Atkinson, R. C. and Shiffrin, R. M. (1968) Human memory: A proposed system and its control processes. In K. W. Spence and J. T. Spence (eds.) *The Psychology of Learning and Motivation* 2. New York: Academic Press. Reprinted in Gardiner. *63*

Baddeley, A. D. (1966) The influence of acoustic and semantic similarity on long-term memory for word sequences. *Quarterly Journal of Experimental Psychology 18*: 302–9. Reprinted in Coltheart (1972). *62*

Baddeley, A. D. and Patterson, K. (1971) The relation between long-term and short-term memory. *British Medical Bulletin 27*: 237–42. *61*

Barnes, J. M. and Underwood, B. J. (1959) 'Fate' of first-list associations in transfer theory. *Journal of Experimental Psychology 58*: 97–105. Reprinted in Slamecka (1967). *127*

Bartlett, F. C. (1932) *Remembering: A Study in Experimental and Social Psychology*. Cambridge: Cambridge University Press. *134*

Bousfield, W. A. (1953) The occurrence of clustering in the recall of randomly arranged associates. *Journal of General Psychology 49*: 229–40. Reprinted in Slamecka (1967). *79*

Bower, G. H. (1970) Analysis of a mnemonic device. *American Scientist 58*: 496–510. Reprinted in Coltheart (1972). *112*

Broadbent, D. E. (1971) *Decision and Stress*. London: Academic Press. *63, 133*

Clarke, H. H. (1970) Word association and linguistic theory in J. Lyons (ed.) *New Horizons in Linguistics*. Harmondsworth: Penguin. *30*

Collins, A. M. and Quillian, M. R. (1969) Retrieval time from semantic memory. *Journal of Verbal Learning and Verbal Behavior* 8: 240–47. Reprinted in Gardiner. *38*

Collins, A. M. and Quillian, M. R. (1970) Does category size affect categorization time? *Journal of Verbal Learning and Verbal Behavior* 9: 432–8. *44*

Coltheart, M. (1972) Visual information-processing. In P. C. Dodwell (ed.) *New Horizons in Psychology* 2. Harmondsworth: Penguin. *65*

Conrad, R. (1957) Decay theory of immediate memory. *Nature* 179: 831–2. *120*

Craik, F. I. M. (1970) The fate of primary memory items in free recall. *Journal of Verbal Learning and Verbal Behavior* 9: 143–8. Reprinted in Gardiner. *70*

Craik, F. I. M. and Lockhart, R. S. (1972) Levels of processing: A framework for memory research. *Journal of Verbal Learning and Verbal Behavior* 11: 671–84. *88, 133*

Dallett, K. M. (1964) Implicit mediators in paired-associate learning. *Journal of Verbal Learning and Verbal Behavior* 3: 209–14. *108*

Davis, R., Sutherland, N. S., and Judd, B. R. (1961) Information content in recognition and recall. *Journal of Experimental Psychology* 61: 422–9. *98*

Deese, J. (1965) *The Structure of Associations in Language and Thought*. Baltimore: Johns Hopkins Press. *31, 82*

Glanzer, M. and Meinzer, A. (1967) The effects of intralist activity on free recall. *Journal of Verbal Learning and Verbal Behavior* 6: 928–35. *70*

Glanzer, M. and Razel, M. (1974) The size of the unit in short-term memory storage. *Journal of Verbal Learning and Verbal Behavior* 13: 114–31. *73*

Greene, J. (1972) *Psycholinguistics*. Harmondsworth: Penguin. *22*

Haber, R. N. and Haber, R. B. (1964) Eidetic imagery: 1. Frequency *Perceptual and Motor Skills* 19: 131–8. *57, 95, 109*

Hyde, J. S. and Jenkins, J. J. (1973) Recall of words as a function of semantic, graphic, and syntactic orienting tasks. *Journal of Verbal Learning and Verbal Behavior* 12: 471–80. *88*

Jenkins, J. B. and Dallenbach, K. M. (1924) Obliviscence during sleep and waking. *American Journal of Psychology* 35: 605–12. *120, 124*

Jenkins, J. J. and Russell, W. A. (1952) Associative clustering during recall. *Journal of Abnormal and Social Psychology* 47: 818–21. *81, 82*

Kausler, D. H. (1974) *Psychology of Verbal Learning and Memory*. New York: Academic Press. *33*

Keppel, G. and Underwood, B. J. (1962) Proactive inhibition in short-term retention of single items. *Journal of Verbal Learning and Verbal Behavior 1*: 153–61. Reprinted in Postman and Keppel (1969) and Slamecka (1967). *122*

Landauer, T. K. and Freedman, J. L. (1968) Information retrieval from long-term memory: Category size and recognition time. *Journal of Verbal Learning and Verbal Behavior* 7: 291–5. *41*

Luria, A. R. and Vinogradova, O. S. (1959) An objective investigation of the dynamics of semantic systems. *British Journal of Psychology 50*: 89–105. *33*

Melton, A. W. (1963) Implications of short-term memory for a general theory of memory. *Journal of Verbal Learning and Verbal Behavior 2*: 1–21. Reprinted in Slamecka (1967). *119*

Miller, G. A. (1956) The magical number seven plus or minus two: Some limits on our capacity for processing information. *Psychological Review 63*: 81–97. Reprinted in Slamecka (1967). *77, 80*

Morton, J. (1970) A functional model for memory. In D. A. Norman (ed.) *Models of Human Memory*. New York: Academic Press. *67*

Noble, C. E. (1963) Meaningfulness and familiarity. In C. N. Cofer and B. S. Musgrave (eds.) *Verbal Behavior and Learning*. New York: McGraw Hill. *28*

Osgood, C. E. (1953) *Method and Theory in Experimental Psychology*. New York: Oxford University Press. *26*

Paivio, A. (1971) *Imagery and Verbal Processes*. New York: Holt, Rinehart and Winston. *49, 106, 110, 113*

Paivio, A., Yuille, J. C. and Madigan, S. (1968) Concreteness, imagery, and meaningfulness values for 925 nouns. *Journal of Experimental Psychology, Monograph Supplement 76* (1, pt. 2). *51*

Penfield, W. (1958) *The Excitable Cortex in Conscious Man*. New York: Thomas. *53*

Popper, K. R. (1959) *The Logic of Scientific Discovery*. New York: Basic Books. *14*

Postman, L. and Keppel, G. (1970) *Norms of Word Association*. New York: Academic Press. *31*

Postman, L. and Underwood, B. J. (1973) Critical issues in interference theory. *Memory and Cognition 1*: 19–40. *127*

Richardson, A. (1969) *Mental Imagery*. London: Routledge and Kegan Paul. *55*

Schaeffer, B. and Wallace, R. (1970) The comparison of word meanings. *Journal of Experimental Psychology* 86: 144–52. Reprinted in Gardiner. *45*

Shepard, R. N. and Metzler, J. (1971) Mental rotation of three-dimensional objects. *Science* (New York) *171*: 701–3. *55*

Sperling, G. (1960) The information available in brief visual presentations. *Psychological Monographs: General and Applied* 74: 1–29. *64*

Standing, L., Conezio, J. and Haber, R. N. (1970) Perception and memory for pictures: Single-trial learning of 2560 visual stimuli. *Psychonomic Science* 19: 73–4. *109*

Talland, G. A. (1968) *Disorders of Memory and Learning*. Harmondsworth: Penguin. *129*

Tulving, E. (1962) Subjective organisation in free recall of 'unrelated' words. *Psychological Review* 69: 344–54. Reprinted in Slamecka (1967). *84, 85*

Tulving, E. (1966) Subjective organisation and effects of repetition in multi-trial free-recall learning. *Journal of Verbal Learning and Verbal Behavior* 5: 193–7. Reprinted in Gardiner. *86*

Tulving, E. (1968) Theoretical issues in free recall. In T. R. Dixon and D. L. Horton (eds.) *Verbal Behavior and General Behavior Theory*. Englewood Cliffs, New Jersey: Prentice Hall. *77, 81, 128*

Tulving, E. (1972) Episodic and semantic memory. In E. Tulving and W. Donaldson (eds.) *Organization of Memory*. New York: Academic Press. *61*

Tulving, E. (1974) Cue-dependent forgetting. *American Scientist* 62: 74–82. *128*

Tulving, E. and Osler, S. (1968) Effectiveness of retrieval cues in memory for words. *Journal of Experimental Psychology* 77: 593–601. Reprinted in Gardiner. *91, 93, 102*

Tulving, E. and Pearlstone, Z. (1966) Availability versus accessibility of information in memory for words. *Journal of Verbal Learning and Verbal Behavior* 5: 381–91. Reprinted in Gardiner. *80, 90*

Watkins, M. J. (1974) Concept and measurement of primary memory. *Psychological Bulletin* 81: 695–711. *71*

Waugh, N. and Norman, D. A. (1965) Primary memory. *Psychological Review* 72: 89–104. Reprinted in Gardiner, and Slamecka (1967). *67, 72, 73, 121*

Wickens, D. D. (1972) Characteristics of word encoding. In A. W. Melton and E. Martin (eds.) *Coding Processes in Human Memory*. Washington, DC: Winston and Sons. *124*

Williams, M. (1970) *Brain Damage and the Mind*. Harmondsworth: Penguin. *16, 129*

Index

141

142

Other books from Methuen

ATTRIBUTES OF MEMORY   *Peter Herriot*

An up-to-date review of experimental research on memory, which takes as its unifying theme the concept of coding by attributes – in opposition to the currently dominant model of information flow from short-term to long-term memory stores.

University Paperback

Forthcoming:

READINGS IN HUMAN MEMORY
                              Edited by John Gardiner

These readings reflect the enormous impetus given to research in human memory following the adoption of information processing concepts from computer science. They form a companion volume to Peter Herriot's *Attributes of Memory*.

University Paperback

Also by John Gardiner:

Essential Psychology A9
FIRST EXPERIMENTS IN PSYCHOLOGY
                    John M. Gardiner and Zofia Kaminska

Psychology, especially those topics discussed in Unit A of this series, proceeds largely by experiment. This book introduces experimental principles and techniques by way of practice and experience. The main part presents set experiments, while in the final part readers are encouraged to design new ones of their own.

Essential Psychology A1
AN INTRODUCTION TO PSYCHOLOGICAL SCIENCE
Basic processes in the analysis of behaviour   *David Legge*

This is the introductory volume to Unit A of *Essential Psychology*, which is concerned with the classical area of psychology – how people perceive, learn, memorize, develop and use skills, and with the parts of the brain concerned with these processes. This book introduces the major topics in basic psychology and relates them to other aspects of psychology including the main areas of specialist professional practice.

All these titles are available from your usual bookseller.

In case of difficulty, please write to the Publishers: Methuen & Co. Ltd., Marketing Department, North Way, Andover, Hampshire SP10 5BE.